D0683138

# Brecon Beacons

Compiled by
Tom Hutton

## Acknowledgements

I'm always grateful to the staff of the Brecon Beacons National Park for working so hard to keep such a wonderful place, wonderful. My thanks also go to my partner, Steph, for her love and support, and to Du, for her companionship. Walks wouldn't be the same without her.

| | |
|---|---|
| **Text:** | Tom Hutton |
| **Photography:** | Tom Hutton |
| **Editorial:** | Ark Creative (UK) Ltd |
| **Design:** | Ark Creative (UK) Ltd |

ISBN: 978-1-85458-532-5

While every care has been taken to ensure the accuracy of the route directions, the publishers cannot accept responsibility for errors or omissions, or for changes in details given. The countryside is not static: hedges and fences can be removed, stiles can become gates, field boundaries can alter, footpaths can be rerouted and changes in ownership can result in the closure or diversion of some concessionary paths. Also, paths that are easy and pleasant for walking in fine conditions may become slippery, muddy and difficult in wet weather, while stepping stones across rivers and streams may become impassable. If you find an inaccuracy in either the text or maps, please write to Crimson Publishing at the address below.

First published 2005. Revised and reprinted 2007, 2008, 2011.

This edition first published in Great Britain 2011 by Crimson Publishing and reprinted with amendments in 2015.
Crimson Publishing,
19-21C Charles Street,
Bath, BA1 1HX
www.pathfinderwalks.co.uk

Printed in Singapore. 5/15

**Front cover:** The northern slopes of the Black Mountains
**Previous page:** Talybont Reservoir from Tor y Foel

# Contents

# Keymap

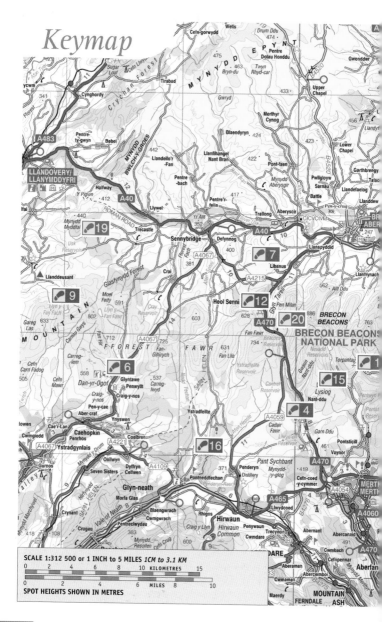

SCALE 1:312 500 or 1 INCH to 5 MILES 1CM to 3.1 KM

0    2    4    6    8    10 KILOMETRES    15

0         2         4         6    MILES    8         10

SPOT HEIGHTS SHOWN IN METRES

# *At-a-glance*

| 1 | 2 | 3 | 4 |
|---|---|---|---|
|  |  |  |  |
| *Blaen-y-glyn* | *Castle Meadows* | *St Mary's Vale* | *Coed Taf Fawr* |

| | | | |
|---|---|---|---|
| • Woodland trails<br>• waterfalls<br>• riverside paths<br>• wagtails | • Riverside path<br>• scenic meadows<br>• castle ruin<br>• Usk Bridge | • Woodland trail<br>• riverside path<br>• woodland wildlife<br>• open hillside | • Woodland<br>• cascading rivers<br>• playground<br>• mountain views |

| Walk Distance | Walk Distance | Walk Distance | Walk Distance |
|---|---|---|---|
| 1½ miles (2.4km) | 1½ miles (2.4km) | 1¾ miles (2.8km) | 2 miles (3.2km) |
| **Time** | **Time** | **Time** | **Time** |
| 1 hour | 1 hour | 1 hour | 1 hour |
| **Refreshments** | **Refreshments** | **Refreshments** | **Refreshments** |
| None | Bridge End Inn, Llanfoist. Abergavenny has plenty of cafés | None | Café at the visitor centre |

| | | | |
|---|---|---|---|
| Woodland; tree roots; muddy paths; slippery rocks | Clear paths; grassy meadows; riverside path; castle ruins; museum | Woodland; tree roots; stream crossings; slippery rocks; steep climb; open hillsides | Forest trails; muddy paths; tree roots; stream crossing; waterfalls |

| p. 16 | p. 20 | p. 24 | p. 28 |
|---|---|---|---|
| Walk Completed  | Walk Completed | Walk Completed | Walk Completed |

**5** **6** **7** **8**

*Tor y Foel*　　*Craig-y-nos and the Tawe Valley*　　*Mynydd Illtud*　　*Gilwern Wharf and the Clydach Gorge*

| | | | |
|---|---|---|---|
| • Mountain scenery<br>• stunning views<br>• upland birds<br>• large reservoir | • Stepping stones<br>• riverside trail<br>• country park<br>• cave visit | • Great views<br>• nature reserve<br>• Iron Age fort<br>• mountain centre | • Canal heritage<br>• old tram road<br>• pretty woodland<br>• riverside path |
| **Walk Distance**<br>2¼ miles (3.6km)<br>**Time**<br>2 hours<br>**Refreshments**<br>None | **Walk Distance**<br>2½ miles (4km)<br>**Time**<br>1½ hours<br>**Refreshments**<br>The walk passes the Gwyn Arms. New café at the visitor centre | **Walk Distance**<br>2¾ miles (4.4km)<br>**Time**<br>1½ hours<br>**Refreshments**<br>Excellent restaurant at the mountain centre | **Walk Distance**<br>2¼ miles (3.6km)<br>**Time**<br>1½ hours<br>**Refreshments**<br>The Corn Exchange at Gilwern. The Bridge Inn is also a few minutes from the route at the end |
| Grassy tracks; muddy paths; views; steep descent | Muddy paths; riverside; stepping stones; field paths; road crossings | Grassy tracks; views; ponds; Iron Age fort | Canal towpath; steep muddy track; quiet lanes; grassy footpaths; woodland path |

**p.32**　　**p. 36**　　**p. 40**　　**p. 44**

Walk Completed ☐　　Walk Completed ☐　　Walk Completed ☐　　Walk Completed ☐

**9**

*Llyn y Fan Fach*

**10**

*The Llangattock Escarpment*

**11**

*The Blorenge*

**12**

*Craig Cerrig-gleisiad*

---

| | | | |
|---|---|---|---|
| • Mountain scenery<br>• ledgend of the lake<br>• fish hatchery<br>• mountain wildlife | • Fantastic views<br>• old quarries<br>• towering cliffs<br>• industrial history | • Wonderful views<br>• grouse moor<br>• hang-gliders<br>• famous grave | • Nature reserve<br>• glacial landscape<br>• craggy cliffs<br>• Alpine flora |

**Walk Distance**
2½ miles (4km)
**Time**
1½ hours
**Refreshments**
None

**Walk Distance**
3¼ miles (5.2km)
**Time**
2 hours
**Refreshments**
None

**Walk Distance**
3½ miles (5.6km)
**Time**
2 hours
**Refreshments**
None

**Walk Distance**
4 miles (6.4km)
Shorter version
1¼ miles (1.9km)
**Time**
2 hours (1 hour
for shorter version)
**Refreshments**
None

---

Rocky track;
lakeside mountain
views

Grassy tracks;
steep paths;
spectacular cliff
scenery; views;
industrial history

Grassy tracks;
muddy paths;
views; rocky
summit; quiet road
section

Rocky escarpment
and cliffs; steep
climb; clear tracks;
muddy paths;
stream crossings.
*Shorter route:
rocky escarpment
and cliffs; muddy
paths;
some stiles*

---

**p. 48**

**p. 52**

**p. 56**

**p. 60**

Walk
Completed ☐

Walk
Completed ☐

Walk
Completed ☐

Walk
Completed ☐

| 13 | 14 | 15 | 16 |
|---|---|---|---|
|  |  |  |  |
| *Grwyne Fawr Reservoir* | *Goytre Wharf and Pentre Hill* | *The Taf Fechan Forest* | *The Waterfalls Walk* |

| | | | |
|---|---|---|---|
| • Huge dam<br>• mountain tracks<br>• dippers<br>• picnic spot | • Woodland trails<br>• canal towath<br>• country inn<br>• pleasure boats | • Upland reservoir<br>• riverside path<br>• forest trails<br>• fine views | • Spectacular falls<br>• river birdlife<br>• walk under fall<br>• enormous cave |
| **Walk Distance**<br>4 miles (6.4km)<br>**Time**<br>2 hours<br>**Refreshments**<br>None | **Walk Distance**<br>4½ miles (7.2km)<br>**Time**<br>2 hours<br>**Refreshments**<br>Restaurant at the start and the Goose and Cuckoo public house | **Walk Distance**<br>4 miles (6.4km)<br>**Time**<br>2 hours<br>**Refreshments**<br>None | **Walk Distance**<br>5 miles (8km)<br>**Time**<br>2 hours<br>**Refreshments**<br>None |
| Clear rocky paths; grassy meadows; open moorland; reservoir; riverside road; picnic areas | Woodland trails; muddy field paths; meadows; canal towpath | Woodland; riverside paths; boggy moorland | Slippery rock; roots; steep steps; muddy tracks; forest trails; waterfalls |

p.64     p. 69     p. 73     p. 78

Walk Completed ☐    Walk Completed ☐    Walk Completed ☐    Walk Completed ☐

| **17** | **18** | **19** | **20** |

| *The Sugar Loaf* | *The Cat's Back and Black Hill* | *The Usk Reservoir* | *Pen y Fan* |

| • Mountain scenery | • Rocky ridge | • Woodland trails | • Beacons high point |
| • rocky summit | • mountain scenery | • lakeside paths | • unbelievable views |
| • Incredible views | • great views | • lovely views | • memorial |
| • mountain birdlife | • deep valley | • easy walking | • mountain scenery |

| **Walk Distance** | **Walk Distance** | **Walk Distance** | **Walk Distance** |
| 4½ miles (7.2km) | 5 miles (8km) | 5½ miles (8.8km) | 5 miles (8km) |
| **Time** | **Time** | **Time** | **Time** |
| 3 hours | 3 hours | 2½ hours | 3 hours |
| **Refreshments** | **Refreshments** | **Refreshments** | **Refreshments** |
| None | None | None | There's often a snack van in the car park |

| Grassy mountain paths; rocky summit | Rocky ridge; open moorland; steep valley path; narrow lane | Forest tracks; lakeside paths; tarmac lane | Rocky paths; steep climbs; mountain summits |

| **p. 83** | **p. 88** | **p.93** | **p. 98** |

| Walk Completed ☐ | Walk Completed ☐ | Walk Completed ☐ | Walk Completed ☐ |

# Introduction

This is a walking book designed specifically for non-walkers; if that isn't a contradiction in terms. The 20 easy-to-follow routes have been carefully chosen to encourage inexperienced walkers to pull on a pair of boots and take their first few bold steps out into the joys and wonders of the great outdoors. To start with, on short and gentle strolls that the whole family will manage with ease and then, as the book progresses, on slightly more demanding jaunts that get deep into the heart of the wonderful Brecon Beacons' countryside but still won't take you more than half a day to complete.

*Pen y Fan in winter*

Each outing has been selected for a specific reason; either because it visits a site of interest, or because it offers opportunities to see fascinating flora or fauna that otherwise wouldn't be seen, or, more often than not, just because it opens up some of the finest landscapes in the National Park and provides the walker with the kind of views that couldn't possibly be enjoyed from any car park or picnic site.

It's a book written with families in mind; each walk containing useful and interesting information about the area that it explores as well as including a specific question that will hopefully encourage the youngsters to play an active and inquisitive role in the day's proceedings.

The walks are graded by length and difficulty to allow the reader to choose the right one for the day and for the age and fitness level of the party that they are walking with. The easiest ones cross reasonably level ground on clear and easy-to-follow paths but this is very mountainous countryside and walks of this grade are hard to come by. Therefore most of the outings involve at least some uphill walking; the tougher ones, nearer the end of the book, a fair bit. *Walk 20* is an ascent of the highest mountain in the National Park; a demanding ramble, yes, but also a worthwhile objective to work towards. Build up your fitness levels and experience gradually and never be afraid to back off a walk if anybody in the party is struggling or, as so often happens in these parts, the weather starts to deteriorate.

While specialist equipment isn't really necessary for any of these walks, a lot of them cross some very rough ground, as is often the way in mountainous terrain, so a pair of walking boots and some thick socks will certainly make things a lot more comfortable. On all but the shortest routes it's worth carrying a bottle of water and a few snacks. More than anything, these will offer comfort and encouragement to anybody who gets tired or cold.

## *The Brecon Beacons National Park*
Covering an area of over 500 square miles, the Brecon Beacons National Park is actually made up of four distinct separate mountain ranges as well as some easier ground to the south and three isolated peaks that surround the small town of Abergavenny.

In the east, the Black Mountains comprise of five distinct broad ridges, linked at their northern end by some peaty moorland and an impressive north-facing escarpment that casts a lengthy shadow over the wide expanse of the Wye Valley. *Walk 13*, a straightforward sortie around the head of the Grwyne Fawr Valley, penetrates deep into the heart of this range, while *Walk 18* traces the Cat's Back along its easternmost reaches. *Walks 10, 11* and *18* all offer fantastic views of the range.

South of these hills are the three Abergavenny peaks. The highest, the Sugar Loaf, is one of the most distinctive mountains in the area and is explored in *Walk 17*, while across the Usk Valley stands the imposing bulk of the mighty Blorenge, a lofty peak that's easily scaled by *Walk 11*. The third, Ysgyryd Fawr isn't covered in the book but is well worth a visit.

The skyline in the centre of the National Park is dominated by the Brecon Beacons themselves, whose dramatic profiles are at their most impressive when viewed from the north on *Walk 7*; an easy stroll across Mynydd Illtud Common. Their southern slopes present a friendlier face to walkers who follow *Walk 4* and *Walk 15*, and their summits are crested by the toughest route in the book on *Walk 20*.

The Cat's Back, Olchon Valley, Black Mountains

Abergavenny Castle

West of the true Beacons is Fforest Fawr, once the hunting ground of kings, now a windswept cluster of grassy topped peaks that don't lend themselves to easy family walking. An exception is Craig Cerrig-gleisiad – a National Nature Reserve. Its deep hollows and craggy tops are examined close-up on *Walk 12*. South of these mountains, the rivers have carved deep gorges for themselves and it's here that the most impressive waterfalls in the National Park are found. *Walk 16* takes a ramble around these.

The far west is known as the Mynydd Du or Black Mountain (singular) and this is probably the most remote part of the National Park, comprising of mile after mile of austere moorland that sees far fewer visitors than the other areas. Even this forbidding landscape has its weaknesses though, and *Walk 9* gets deep into its bosom with minimum effort, as it climbs to the scenic and now legendary Llyn y Fan Fach, a beautiful mountain tarn nestled beneath towering cliffs. *Walk 6* skirts around the edge of the wilderness – starting at the lovely Craig-y-nos Country Park – and *Walk 19* allows some clear views of its magnificent skyline from the wooded shores of this area's largest stretch of water.

From gurgling brook to turbulent river, from sheltered glade to wind-swept summit and from rolling meadow to sprawling forest, there really is something here for everybody. History abounds, wildlife ekes a living out of every nook and cranny and even the scars of the industrial revolution have left a unique yet attractive mark on this very special corner of Wales. The aim of this book is to help you to enjoy it.

This book includes a list of waypoints alongside the description of the walk, so that you can enjoy the full benefits of gps should you wish to.

For more information on using your gps, read the *Pathfinder® Guide GPS for Walkers*, by gps teacher and navigation trainer, Clive Thomas (ISBN 978-0-7117-4445-5).

For essential information on map reading and basic navigation, read the *Pathfinder® Guide Map Reading Skills* by outdoor writer, Terry Marsh (ISBN 978-0-7117-4978-8). Both titles are available in bookshops or can be ordered online at www.pathfinderwalks.co.uk

# Blaen-y-glyn

- ■ Woodland trails
- ■ waterfalls
- ■ riverside paths
- ■ wagtails and dippers

*walk 1*

*This is a lovely and straightforward walk through pretty woodland and along the banks of a wonderful mountain stream, peppered with spectacular cascades and waterfalls. The going does get quite rough in some places and a few sections of the path can be quite muddy. Boots are definitely recommended for keeping feet dry.*

Cascades are a regular feature on this walk

# walk 1

**START** Pont Blaen-y-glyn

**DISTANCE** 1½ miles (2.4km)

**TIME** 1 hour

**PARKING** Car park next to the bridge

**ROUTE FEATURES** Woodland; tree roots; muddy paths; slippery rocks

**GPS WAYPOINTS**
- SO 063 170
- Ⓐ SO 059 173
- Ⓑ SO 060 174

**PUBLIC TRANSPORT** Summer bus service from Brecon and Talybont on Usk

**REFRESHMENTS** None

**PUBLIC TOILETS** None

**PLAY AREA** None

**ORDNANCE SURVEY MAPS** Explorer OL12 (Brecon Beacons National Park – Western & Central areas), Landranger 160 (Brecon Beacons)

Walk up through the car park, and around a barrier to join a good firm track that leads into the woods. Continue easily upwards past some wonderful moss-covered tumbledown walls and across a few small streams.

Keep heading in the same direction until you cross a small bridge that spans a turbulent stream, with some small cascades above and below you Ⓐ. Turn left after the bridge and start heading upstream with the stream on your left. As the path bends to the right and starts to climb very steeply, you can bear slightly left to follow the stream into an almost magical grotto with a wonderful waterfall directly ahead. *The path is usually muddy here and the rocks are very slippery.*

**?** *Pont is the Welsh word for bridge. How many bridges do you cross on the walk?*

Return to the woodland path, where if you wish, you can turn left to continue steeply uphill to view further waterfalls. If you do not fancy the steep climb, turn right to retrace your steps back to the main path, where you need to turn left for a few paces to a fork, with some ruined buildings to your left. Turn right at the fork and drop down to a stile that leads to a bridge over the Caerfanell River Ⓑ. Here you'll get your first sighting of the

*Fast flowing rivers and streams like the Caerfanell are great places to spot wildlife. There are many different species of birds and mammals making the banks and surrounding woodland their home. These include **otters**, which are very secretive and seldom seen, and **mink**, which are not indigenous but have spread across most of the UK.

spectacular Caerfanell Falls.

The walk continues over the bridge but before crossing, it is possible to make your way up the rocky bank towards the falls to get a better view. *Care is needed; the rock*

Caerfanell waterfall

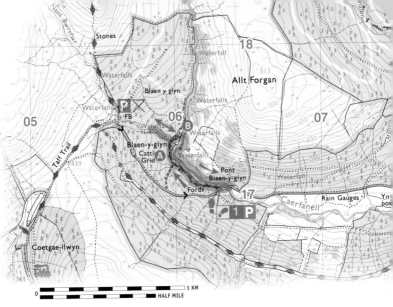

*is usually quite slippery.* Now cross the bridge and turn left to follow a narrow and often muddy path upstream a few metres to look at the top of the falls. Return to the bridge and keep straight ahead, now with the stream to your right. Navigation is easy from here as all you need to do is follow the river-bank down, enjoying the many rapids and cascades as you go.

There's plenty to look out for. Dippers are frequently seen dashing from rock to rock in the stream and you may also spot grey wagtails or even

*Backlit leaves and rocks, Blaen-y-glyn*

the odd heron. *The path is tricky in places, with a few steep and slippery sections that need to be treated with care.* Eventually the going eases and you're left with an easy short stroll to the bridge. Go through the kissing-gate and turn right to cross the river and return to the car park. ■

# Castle Meadows

- Riverside path
- scenic meadow
- castle ruin
- Usk Bridge

*An easy and enjoyable stroll; suitable for the whole family and easily accessible by public transport. Abergavenny makes a great base for exploration; particularly of the Black Mountains area. This walk traces the banks of the mighty River Usk offering good chances to spot wildlife, and great views of the surrounding mountains.*

Castle meadows and the River Usk

# walk **2**

**START** Abergavenny bus station

**DISTANCE** 1$\frac{1}{2}$ miles (2.4km)

**TIME** 1 hour

**PARKING** Pay and Display at the start

**ROUTE FEATURES** Clear paths; grassy meadows; riverside path; castle ruins; museum

**GPS WAYPOINTS**
SO 301 140
Ⓐ SO 299 138
Ⓑ SO 291 140
Ⓒ SO 297 137
Ⓓ SO 300 136

**PUBLIC TRANSPORT** Buses and trains to Abergavenny

**REFRESHMENTS** The walk can be broken up by visiting the Bridge End Inn, Llanfoist, which is a few minutes from Ⓑ . Abergavenny has plenty of cafés

**PUBLIC TOILETS** At the start

**PLAY AREA** None

**ORDNANCE SURVEY MAPS** Explorer OL13 (Brecon Beacons National Park – Eastern area), Landranger 161 (The Black Mountains)

Walk past the information centre and out of the car park onto the road. Turn right and then cross the road immediately to turn left, up Mill Street, with the Shahi Indian restaurant on your right. As the road veers left, keep ahead until the road ends and a path leads you down to Castle Meadows. The castle walls can be seen on top of the large hillock on the right.

> ✳ Little more than a tumbledown ruin in a prominent position overlooking the River Usk, **Abergavenny Castle** was originally founded in the 11th century. The stone construction that we see now was started in the later 1100s by the Normans and added to until it reached its most impressive condition during the 13th and 14th century. It was visited by King John in 1215. Charles I ordered its demolition in 1645 when it became a good source for local building stone.

Keep straight ahead to a gate that leads out onto the meadows Ⓐ. Go through this and bear right to follow a muddy path towards a wooden bridge, keeping a boggy dyke to your right. Cross the bridge and keep heading in the same direction to cross the meadows until you reach a well-surfaced track that crosses your path. Keep ahead here, still on the muddy path, and continue until you reach the far side of the meadows, where you'll clearly see the road ahead Ⓑ.

Abergavenny Castle

Turn left to keep the wall to your right and walk down to join a well-surfaced trail at an elaborate kissing-gate. Turn left onto this trail and follow it along the banks of the river with fine views over the water to the steep slopes of the Blorenge mountain. After a few minutes, you'll notice some sandy cliffs on the opposite bank. In summer, this makes a great nesting area for sand martins, which burrow into the bank and can be seen catching flies above the river.

**?** *What is the name for Abergavenny in Welsh?*

Continue until the main path veers to the left **C** but keep straight ahead, again on a muddy path, to follow the riverbank a little farther. Soon you'll cross a wooden footbridge over a small tributary stream and then, just a few paces farther on, you'll be forced to keep left to follow another stream up towards another footbridge **D**. This stream is actually the Gavenny River, from which the town takes its name.

Do not cross this bridge, which is now on your right. Instead, bear left to join a good path and follow this back to another bridge, where you bear right, through a gate. Follow the grassy track to the gate at the edge of the meadows  . To return to the car park, keep straight ahead retracing your outward steps. *To visit the castle and museum, keep left now, with the castle walls above you to your right, and continue up to the gates on the right. When you've finished, retrace your steps back down to the steps above the gate and turn left to retrace your outward tracks back to the car park.*

Waymark near Abergavenny Castle

# St Mary's Vale

■ Woodland trail ■ woodland wildlife
■ riverside path ■ open hillside

One of the prettiest wooded valleys in the area, St Mary's Vale provides enjoyable and energetic walking on the outskirts of Abergavenny. In spring, the sound of birdsong fills the air and in autumn the colours are truly wonderful. Some of the paths can be difficult to follow in late summer when the bracken is high.

*Open hillside above St Mary's Vale*

# walk 3

**START** Head of narrow lane near Abergavenny

**DISTANCE** 1¾ miles (2.8km)

**TIME** 1 hour

**PARKING** At the start

**ROUTE FEATURES** Woodland; tree roots; stream crossings; slippery rocks; steep climb; open hillsides

**GPS WAYPOINTS**
SO 283 161
Ⓐ SO 281 164
Ⓑ SO 278 167
Ⓒ SO 276 172
Ⓓ SO 279 170

**PUBLIC TRANSPORT** None

**REFRESHMENTS** None

**PUBLIC TOILETS** None

**PLAY AREA** None

**ORDNANCE SURVEY MAPS** Explorer OL13 (Brecon Beacons National Park – Eastern area), Landranger 161 (The Black Mountains)

Walk out of the car park and turn left for a few paces to a fork. Keep left to walk along a gravel drive that runs beneath a house to a gate. Go through the gate and drop down a clear track to the stream at the bottom of the valley. Cross the flagstone bridge Ⓐ but do not be tempted over the stile on the left, instead, keep the stream to your right and follow it up into the woods.

Cross a narrow channel so that you are walking with the stream on both sides and then cross it again so that the stream is now on your right. You are on a clear, muddy jeep track that continues up into woods. Stay with this until it makes a sharp left hairpin turn by a broader pool in the stream Ⓑ. Cross the stream here and you will see two paths forking up the hillside. Take the left-hand one, and climb steeply, on a clear but narrow path away from the stream. Eventually the path levels at an open glade, just short of some open hillside, with a fence corner to the right and a huge oak tree marking a junction of tracks Ⓒ.

Bear left, around the oak tree, and walk beneath a broken branch on a narrow path that soon meets a brook. Keep the brook to your left and continue for a few paces to an

> **?** What is the name of the woodland that you are walking in?

obvious crossing point on the edge of open ground. There's a small sign pointing right but you need to keep straight ahead on a clear track that swings slightly right and continues up through the heather and bilberry. You'll soon come to a three-way fork, with an animal drinking trough to your left and a metal drain cover to your right. Ignore the path that leads right to a stile, and instead keep ahead on a narrow path to eventually merge with a clearer track that comes in from your left.

*Autumn birch trees*

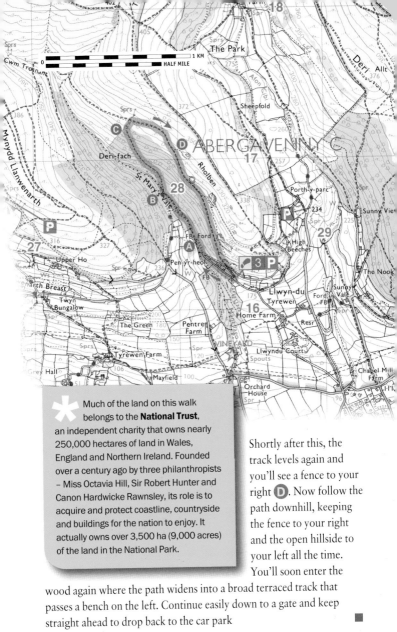

Shortly after this, the track levels again and you'll see a fence to your right **D**. Now follow the path downhill, keeping the fence to your right and the open hillside to your left all the time. You'll soon enter the wood again where the path widens into a broad terraced track that passes a bench on the left. Continue easily down to a gate and keep straight ahead to drop back to the car park ▪

# Coed Taf Fawr

- Woodland
- cascading rivers
- adventure playground
- mountain views

*Garwnant Forest Park is one of the real highlights of the area, especially for families, and this walk, an easy waymarked stroll from the superbly equipped visitor centre, is a great introduction. Known as the Wern Walk, it follows the long distance Taff Trail past the derelict buildings of Wern Farm before climbing up onto a broad forest track for an easy return leg.*

Derelict building, Coed Taf Fawr

**START** Garwnant
Forest Park

**DISTANCE** 2 miles (3.2km)

**TIME** 1 hour

**PARKING** Pay and Display
at the start

**ROUTE FEATURES** Forest
trails; muddy paths; tree
roots; stream crossing;
waterfalls

**GPS WAYPOINTS**
SO 002 131
Ⓐ SO 001 138
Ⓑ SO 002 139
Ⓒ SN 999 143
Ⓓ SN 999 131

**PUBLIC TRANSPORT** Buses
between Brecon and
Merthyr Tydfil, also
summer Beacons Bus
services

**REFRESHMENTS** Café at
the visitor centre

**PUBLIC TOILETS** At the
start

**PLAY AREA** Elaborate play
area at the start

**ORDNANCE SURVEY MAPS**
Explorer OL12 (Brecon
Beacons National Park
– Western & Central
areas), Landranger 160
(Brecon Beacons)

From the visitor centre, follow the clearly signed exit for cars, which follows a well-surfaced forest track out of the far end of the car park. Where this turns right at a barrier, keep straight ahead to continue on another forest track (waymarked Taff Trail). Now follow this trail easily along, through a variety of different woodland, until you reach the derelict buildings of Wern Farm Ⓐ.

**? What is special about evergreen trees?**

Keep these to your left and continue, now on a narrow and sometimes muddy track. A few more minutes of easy walking will see you arrive at a small brook crossing and then, shortly after that, you'll come to a crossroads of tracks Ⓑ, where you need to keep straight ahead although the Taff Trail now drops down to the right to carry on up the Taf Fawr Valley towards Brecon.

Keep heading in the same direction and you'll soon come to some tumbledown buildings, where the trail turns sharp left to go uphill. Follow the trail up, with a tumbling brook down to your right, and beyond that, a recently harvested section of woodland stretching away towards Nant-ddu. At the top of this section, you'll meet a broad well-surfaced forest road Ⓒ, and another waymarker post with a green arrow.

Forest track and trees

Turn left onto this and follow it easily along, with good views in all directions. You'll soon cross the bridleway track that you crossed farther down on the way out and then, shortly after that, you'll pass another forest track that dips off to the left. Continue to a junction **D**, where you start to drop into a valley, and bear left here, to start heading downhill with the powerful Garwnant River down to your right. There are some spectacular falls all the way down the river, which soon finishes its journey as it flows into the Afon Taf Fawr, near the Llwyn-on Reservoir.

**✳ Garwnant Forest Park** is a wonderful facility for all the family with waymarked forest walks, family cycle trails and even an adventure playground, which includes a rope course and a toddlers' play area. The visitor centre features interesting displays and has a gift shop, a café that serves great food made from local produce, and a cosy log fire. Cycle hire is also available if you'd rather ride than walk.

There's a narrow path and viewing platform down to the right should you want a closer look. Either way, continue on down until you see a good path on your left that leads you back up to the car park and visitor centre.

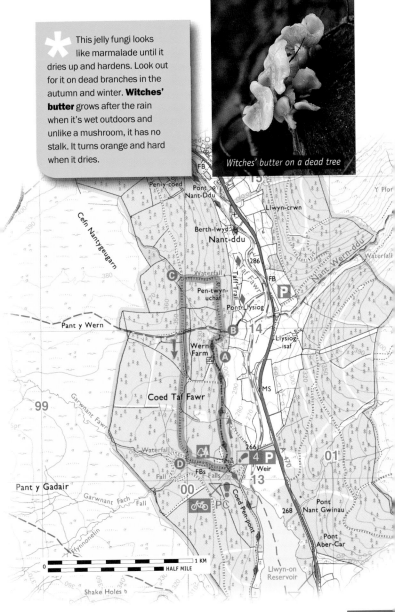

This jelly fungi looks like marmalade until it dries up and hardens. Look out for it on dead branches in the autumn and winter. **Witches' butter** grows after the rain when it's wet outdoors and unlike a mushroom, it has no stalk. It turns orange and hard when it dries.

*Witches' butter on a dead tree*

# Tor y Foel

- Mountain scenery
- stunning views
- upland birds
- large reservoir

A short but wonderfully rewarding walk that crosses some remote moorland before climbing steeply up onto one of the best viewpoints in the National Park. Save this one for a good day as navigation would be awkward in poor visibility and you'd also miss out on the fabulous views across the surrounding countryside.

*walk 5*

Tor y Foel from Allt Lwyd

# walk 5

**START** Small parking area above Talybont-on-Usk

**DISTANCE** 2¼ miles (3.6km)

**TIME** 1½ hour

**PARKING** At the start

**ROUTE FEATURES** Grassy tracks; muddy paths; views; steep descent

**GPS WAYPOINTS**
- SO 109 187
- Ⓐ SO 113 190
- Ⓑ SO 124 193
- Ⓒ SO 114 194

**PUBLIC TRANSPORT** None

**REFRESHMENTS** None

**PUBLIC TOILETS** None

**PLAY AREA** None

**ORDNANCE SURVEY MAPS** Explorer OL13 (Brecon Beacons National Park – Eastern area), Landranger 161 (The Black Mountains)

There's room for a few cars by the gate at the top of the farm drive. From here, walk back the way you came, crossing the drive and keeping the wall to the right, until you reach the corner of the wall, where you'll see an obvious path leading up the steep grassy slopes of the mountain. Take this, but after just a few paces, turn right to join a faint path

> **?** You can see the Talybont Reservoir from the walk; what's the difference between a reservoir and a lake?

that traverses around the hillside, with the wall down to your right. Continue around, rising up slightly to pass the corner of a wood Ⓐ.

Keep heading in the same direction and shortly the heather and bilberry gives way to a fairly thick carpet of bracken, which makes the path difficult to see in mid to late summer. Continue on the same line, with the steep slope to your left and the wall down to your right, and the way ahead should become clear. This is a good place to see mountain birds like the skylark and meadow pipit, which both enjoy this kind of open hillside. In autumn and winter, the area is regularly visited by huge flocks of redwings and fieldfares, which feed off the berries on the numerous small trees that cover the slopes.

Eventually you'll reach flatter ground and the bracken thins out slightly, revealing some peculiar bumpy ground. Bear left here and climb easily up onto the crest of the hill, where you'll meet the obvious main track that runs up the eastern ridge of the mountain **B**.

The **Talybont Reservoir** was originally constructed in the 1930s. It took a considerable work force to build the impressive dam and over 200 people were forced to move home as the valley was flooded. It is now a **Site of Special Scientific Interest (SSSI)** and an important habitat for wildfowl. The dam can be crossed on foot or bicycle.

Turn left onto this and take your time as you pull steeply up towards the top. The views are magnificent, with the Usk Valley down to your right; the mighty river snaking along its floor, and beyond this, the Black Mountains rise up in all their splendour. Southwards you look over the deeply cloven valley of the Dyffryn Crawnon to the austere slopes of Mynydd Llangynidr.

From the top **C**, you'll see right across the Caerfanell Valley to the moorland plateau of Waun Rhydd, towering above the glistening

*Looking over Bwlch-y-waun from Tor y Foel*

waters of the Talybont Reservoir. There's scant shelter at the summit so unless it's a particularly good day, you'll probably want to get moving straight away. Drop down the obvious path, and continue steeply down with great views now over the head of Caerfanell Valley to the outlying peak of Allt Lwyd. Continue all the way back down to the road, where you left the car.

*The Talybont Reservoir and Waun Rydd from Tor y Foel*

# Craig-y-nos and the Tawe Valley

- Stepping stones
- riverside trail
- country park
- cave visit

*walk 6*

*A gem of a walk following the mighty Tawe River from Craig-y-nos Country Park to its confluence with the equally impressive Afon Haffes. The going is easy the whole way round, but some athleticism might be needed to cross the stepping stones over the Afon Haffes.* Note: do not attempt the river crossing after heavy rain, when it can be turbulent and dangerous.

*Bridge over the Afon Tawe, Craig-y-nos Country Park*

**START** Craig-y-nos Country Park

**DISTANCE** 2½ miles (4km)

**TIME** 1½ hours

**PARKING** Pay and Display at the start

**ROUTE FEATURES** Muddy paths; riverside; stepping stones; field paths; road crossings

**GPS WAYPOINTS**

SN 839 155
Ⓐ SN 842 157
Ⓑ SN 842 160
Ⓒ SN 841 167
Ⓓ SN 845 165
Ⓔ SN 848 166
Ⓕ SN 847 162

**PUBLIC TRANSPORT**
Regular bus service between Brecon and Swansea

**REFRESHMENTS** The walk passes the Gwyn Arms. Wonderful new café at the visitor centre

**PUBLIC TOILETS**
At the start

**PLAY AREA** Near the start, where there's also a duck pond. Dan-yr-ogof Showcaves on the walk

**ORDNANCE SURVEY MAPS**
Explorer OL12 (Brecon Beacons National Park – Western & Central areas), Landranger 160 (Brecon Beacons)

Walk down to the bottom left-hand corner of the car park and go through the gap in the wall to the shores of the pool. Turn right here and then bear round to the right to follow the gravel track down and around to a wooden bridge that crosses the Afon Tawe. Cross the bridge and bear left to follow a lovely path upstream with a clearing on your right. Continue into a stand of large pine trees and keep ahead to a path junction by a bridge Ⓐ. Keep left to cross the bridge and then continue along the path, going through a gate and between trees to another gate. Continue alongside the stream to the main road Ⓑ.

Cross the road and hop over the stile opposite to walk up to a stile at the top and then another, that leads onto the drive of Dan-yr-ogof Showcaves. Turn right and follow the metalled drive down to a junction, where you keep straight ahead, over a stile, to continue on a good track. Look for a waymark that directs you leftwards, uphill on a rough track. Follow this to a gate and keep ahead for a few paces and then keep your eyes open for a path to the right. Take this and drop down to the Afon Haffes Ⓒ.

The riverbanks are a jumble of stones and boulders so do your best to cross the river using these and then keep ahead to a gate and stile that lead into a copse of hazel and birch. *(Note: if the river proves too difficult to cross, retrace your steps back to the drive that leads to Dan-yr-ogof caves and drop to the A4067*

*Mute swan and Craig-y-nos Country Park*

*there where you can turn left to rejoin the route at* **D**.) Follow the track easily along, with steep pasture to your left and the copse to your right, to a gate and stile. Cross the stile and turn right onto a clear track which you follow down, over two more stiles, to join another drive, that leads down past Carreg Haffes Farm and on down the A4067 **D**.

Turn left to walk along the broad verge and then, cross to continue in the same direction on the pavement. Turn right, through a kissing-gate, into the churchyard and then follow the path around the back of the church to another kissing-gate. Keep ahead to cross a lane and go through another kissing-gate to walk up a field with an old wall to your right. At the top of this field, bear diagonally right to cross the next to a gate by the houses **E**. Turn left onto the road and drop to cross a bridge before climbing for a few more paces to a kissing-gate on your right.

> ✱ The Victorian **Craig- y-nos Estate** was **originally built in 1840**. In 1878, Adelina Patti, a top opera singer bought the estate and extended both the house and gardens to create a wonderful retreat. After her death in 1919, the house became a hospital. The beautiful grounds are now managed by the Brecon Beacons National Park as a country park with a small but informative visitor centre.

Go through this and follow the wall along to a gate. Open this and keep the wall to your left then pass a huge crater to another gate.

**? What kind of horses are kept in the centre that you walk past?**

Head diagonally upwards to a gate at the top, where you join a sunken bridleway track **F**. Turn right onto this and follow it easily for ½ mile to a gate. Go through this and drop to a small gate on your right, go through it and you'll be back on the banks of the Afon Tawe. Turn left to retrace your steps back to the start ■

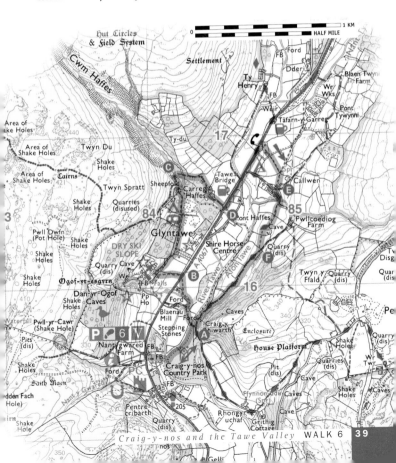

# Mynydd Illtud

- Great views
- nature reserve
- Iron Age hill fort
- mountain centre

*Very easy, yet one of the most rewarding walks in the whole book. It follows undulating grassy tracks across the common land of Mynydd Illtud and terminates on the ramparts of an Iron Age fort offering breathtaking views across the highest mountains in the National Park. Make time to investigate the displays in the mountain centre and to enjoy lunch in the restaurant.*

*Mynydd Illtud and the mountains of Fforest Fawr*

# walk 7

**START** Mountain centre, Libanus

**DISTANCE** 2¾ miles (4.4km)

**TIME** 1½ hours

**PARKING** Pay and Display at the start

**ROUTE FEATURES** Grassy tracks; views; ponds; Iron Age fort

**GPS WAYPOINTS**
- SN 978 262
- Ⓐ SN 984 269
- Ⓑ SN 989 274
- Ⓒ SN 989 280

**PUBLIC TRANSPORT** Beacon Buses summer service from Brecon. Year round buses stop at the bottom of the lane in Libanus, 2km from the start

**REFRESHMENTS** Excellent restaurant at the mountain centre

**PUBLIC TOILETS** At the start

**PLAY AREA** At the start

**ORDNANCE SURVEY MAPS** Explorer OL12 (Brecon Beacons National Park – Western & Central areas), Landranger 160 (Brecon Beacons)

Walk up through the car park, away from the buildings, to a gate that leads out onto the common. There are a few tracks and paths radiating out from here but you need to take the main one, that goes straight ahead, climbing ever so slightly and running parallel with the fence, which is 50 yds below you to your right. This track does get closer to the fence after a few minutes but it then climbs away from it again to a junction Ⓐ, where you should be able to see a pond ahead and to your right. Keep straight ahead here, keeping to the main path rather than dropping to the pond, and continue past the pond, to another junction, just a few metres short of the narrow road.

Bear diagonally right here to drop to the road by a white post that marks a pipeline. Cross the road and bear slightly left to follow a good path that runs along the edge of the common, with a fence to your right. Stay with this and drop to another narrow lane Ⓑ. You can now see Twyn y Gaer, the hill you are going to climb, directly ahead. Cross the road and keep straight ahead to continue along the edge of the common. Shortly, you'll pass a small pond on your right and then, a few paces after this, you'll see a clear track leading uphill towards the summit of the hill.

> **?** Why did the Iron Age people build their settlements on the tops?

Follow this up to the trig point **C**. This is a wonderful viewpoint with Pen y Fan and Corn Du, the highest mountains in the whole of southern Britain, clearly visible. In the distance, you'll make out the dark shapes of the northern slopes of the Black Mountains and due north; you'll see the River Usk snaking along the valley floor beneath your feet.

To return, bear left at the trig point, to drop down the centre of the ridge on a good clear grassy path that leads back to the road. Cross this and follow the waymark to the Mountain Centre. Fork immediately right to a wall corner and then fork left to continue to the top of the hill. Cross the road and keep

**Mynydd Illtud Common** is now a nature reserve, but this area was once common land, as designated by the manorial system introduced by the Normans. This system gave common people certain rights including grazing, fishing, peat digging and removal of stone, mineral and soil. The lord of the manor retained the hunting and shooting rights. Today, common land is mainly used for grazing and recreation, and this is protected by law. Mynydd Illtud is actually owned by the National Park Authority.

*Pen y Fan and Corn Du from Mynydd IlltudFawr*

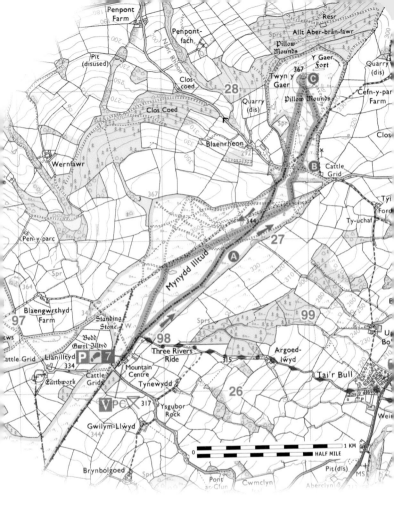

straight ahead again, to follow the main track signed to the Mountain Centre for approximately 100 yds to the junction where you turned right earlier. Bear diagonally right here, onto a clear and dead straight track that climbs slightly. Follow this until the track meets the road, by a large pond. Pass the pond then bear left to walk to the top of the little hill beyond, where you'll meet a good track that you can follow easily downhill back to the Mountain Centre.

# Gilwern Wharf and the Clydach Gorge

- Canal heritage
- old tram road
- pretty woodland
- riverside path

*The area around Gilwern and the Clydach Gorge boasts a fascinating past. This lovely and straightforward walk links the serenity of the Monmouthshire and Brecon Canal with the beautiful wooded valley of the Clydach Gorge, visiting a wonderfully situated church along the way. Although most of the walk is on good paths, the steep climb away from the canal can get muddy.*

*walk 8*

Monmouthshire and Brecon Canal, Gilwern

**START** Gilwern Wharf

**DISTANCE** 2$\frac{1}{4}$ miles (3.6km)

**TIME** 1$\frac{1}{2}$ hours

**PARKING** Gilwern Wharf

**ROUTE FEATURES** Canal
towpath; steep muddy
track; quiet lanes; grassy
footpaths; woodland
path

**GPS WAYPOINTS**
- SO 242 147
- Ⓐ SO 237 152
- Ⓑ SO 232 148
- Ⓒ SN 233 140
- Ⓓ SN 235 139

**PUBLIC TRANSPORT** Buses
from Abergavenny

**REFRESHMENTS** The Corn
Exchange at Gilwern is
close to the start. The
Bridge Inn is also a few
minutes from the route
at the end.

**PUBLIC TOILETS** None

**PLAY AREA** None

**ORDNANCE SURVEY MAPS**
Explorer OL13 (Brecon
Beacons National
Park – Eastern area),
Landranger 161 (The
Black Mountains)

Turn right out of the car park to follow the canal side, shortly passing a bridge with a seat above it that offers great views over the Black Mountains. Continue to the next bridge, number 106, Ⓐ and walk beneath this before crossing the stone stile on your right. Turn right to double back on yourself and cross the bridge – note the old sign – and then follow the track up through trees where it becomes a sunken green lane. Continue up the steep hill until it finally levels and spills onto the road near Llanelly church Ⓑ.

Originally built in the early 13th-century, the church, which occupies a marvellous position with wonderful views, was added to in 1626, possibly funded by the new found local wealth, courtesy of the Clydach Iron Works.

Turn left and walk down the road for a few paces to a stile on the right. Cross this and walk through the middle of the field to another stile, marked 'footpath' and cross

The Monmouthshire and Brecon canal offers 33 miles of waterway weaving through peaceful countryside and wooded glades. Work started on the canal in 1796 before a tunnel was built in 1797 to accommodate the railroad. Gilwern was a busy canal wharf until the advent of the railways in the 1860s and **Aqueduct Cottage** built to house the wharf workers is a good example of industrial worker housing.

this to continue in the same direction. The next stile leads into the corner of a field, where you should keep straight ahead, with the fence to your left, on a slightly raised walkway. Bear right upon reaching the far corner of the field and then cross a stile on the left. Now bear right

*Cascades in the Clydach Gorge*

to keep the hedgerow on your right as you follow the field edge down to a stile. Cross this and turn right onto a broad farm track, which you follow to a narrow lane. Turn left and drop down to a crossroads **C** where you need to keep straight ahead and walk steeply downhill.

Follow the road down past Clydach House and around to the left. At the bottom of the hill, turn left onto a narrow lane that was once the Llam March tram road. Follow this past a row of cottages, once forge workers' dwellings, to the gate to Forge House **D**. Go through the gate and keep straight ahead, with the house to your right. Beyond this, you'll see a narrow path leading away between hedges. Follow this down

The **Llam March tram road** was built in **1809** to link the Clydach Ironworks with the Monmouthshire and Brecon Canal. As you approach the canal, you'll see the Clydach Railroad that runs above you to the left. This is now the road that leads up the gorge, through Maes-y-gwartha. The tram road joins the canal at the Clydach Basin, which is now a boatyard for a narrowboat company.

into woodland and continue along the banks of the Clydach River, still on the line of the old tram road, passing a bridge on the right with wonderful views over a spectacular waterfall. Keep straight ahead at the fork and continue until the narrow wooded track emerges onto a broader track. Turn right and walk downhill, beneath the aquaduct that carries the canal, and then climb the steps on the other side.

**?** *What do you call a bridge that carries water? (Look at the cottage close to this bridge.)*

At the top, turn right onto the canal and follow the towpath back under a bridge to the wharf. ■

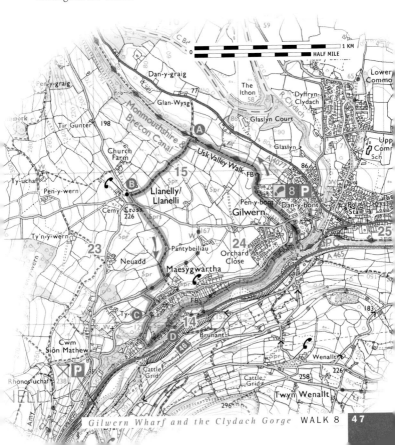

# Llyn y Fan Fach

■ Mountain scenery
■ legend of the lake

■ fish hatchery
■ mountain wildlife

*walk 9*

*The lofty escarpments of the Carmarthen Fan are generally out of bounds to the casual walker but there is one weakness in their defence; an old waterworks track that leads up to Llyn y Fan Fach; often referred to as the 'magic lake' and one of the most scenic spots in the west of the National Park*

Bannau Sir Gaer

| | |
|---|---|
| **START** | Small car park east of Llanddeusant |
| **DISTANCE** | 2½ miles (4km) |
| **TIME** | 1½ hours |
| **PARKING** | At the start, busy on good days, get there early. No charge |
| **ROUTE FEATURES** | Rocky track; lakeside mountain views |

**GPS WAYPOINTS**

- 📷 SN 799 238
- Ⓐ SN 803 230
- Ⓑ SN 803 219

| | |
|---|---|
| **PUBLIC TRANSPORT** | None |
| **REFRESHMENTS** | None |
| **PUBLIC TOILETS** | None |
| **PLAY AREA** | None |

**ORDNANCE SURVEY MAPS**
Explorer OL12 (Brecon Beacons National Park – Western & Central areas), Landranger 160 (Brecon Beacons)

👟 From the car park, join the rocky track and turn right to walk over a bridge and around to the right. Navigation is easy from this point onwards so just stay on the track, with the tumbling Afon Sawdde to your right, and climb gradually upstream until you reach the fish farm at about half distance Ⓐ. The way ahead is blocked by a gate so bear left, through a gap in the wall, and then turn right to follow a narrow and rough path past the old filter beds, which are now used as a fish hatchery so you'll spot plenty of jumping fish.

✱ As well as occupying a stunning position beneath the broken crags of Bannau Sir Gaer, **Llyn y Fan Fach** is also **steeped in myths and legends**, the most famous concerning a magical 'Lady of the Lake'. Legend tells of a local shepherd boy named Rhiwallon who saw the beautiful lady rise from the still waters of the lake. He instantly fell in love with her and asked her to marry him, which she agreed to do so long as he never struck her with iron. They lived happily together. He tended his animals and she produced all kinds of magical healing potions from local herbs and flowers, a skill that she later passed on to their son. Sadly, he did eventually strike her with iron and, true to her word, she returned to the waters of the lake, taking their livestock with her and leaving Rhiwallon a broken man. The son went on to become the first of a line of healers now known as the **Physicians of Myddfai**.

*The Carmarthen Fan and Llyn y Fan Fach*

Continue until the path drops down to join the main track again and follow this on upwards to a bridge that crosses the Afon Sawdde. Keep heading up, with the water now down to your left, and after another few minutes, you'll see a fork, with a grassy path leading off to the left. Take this and follow it around a steep bank to the grassy shores of the reservoir **B**. The steep cliffs ahead are known as the Carmarthen Fans, with the mountain directly above the lake known as Bannau Sir Gaer. Beyond this, and out of sight, the open moorland of the Black Mountain becomes increasingly wild and untrodden.

It's possible to walk most of the way around the lake and there are some great places to enjoy

> **?** How many fish can you see jumping from the hatchery pools?

> **\*** The lady of the lake isn't the only legend concerning the area; just a few miles away, on the other side of the towering cliffs, rises the infant Afon Twrch. **King Arthur** is said to have pursued Twrch Trywth, the magical boar of the Mabinogion, along its banks after chasing it all the way from the Preseli Hills in Pembrokeshire.

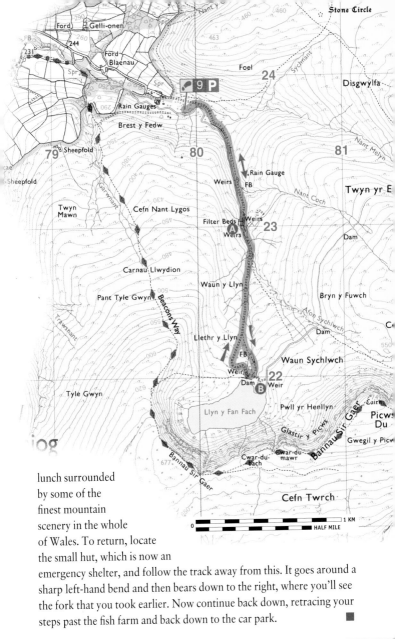

lunch surrounded
by some of the
finest mountain
scenery in the whole
of Wales. To return, locate
the small hut, which is now an
emergency shelter, and follow the track away from this. It goes around a
sharp left-hand bend and then bears down to the right, where you'll see
the fork that you took earlier. Now continue back down, retracing your
steps past the fish farm and back down to the car park.

# The Llangattock Escarpment

- ■ **Fantastic views**
- ■ **old quarries**
- ■ **towering cliffs**
- ■ **industrial history**

*A straightforward ramble that offers some fantastic views as well as an insight into the huge quarrying industry that once dominated the hillsides in this part of Wales. The craggy escarpments of Craig y Cilau are breathtakingly grand and the towering limestone cliffs are home to all kinds of wildlife.*

*Crickhowell from the Llangattock Escarpment*

# walk 10

**START** Car park on Llangattock Escarpment

**DISTANCE** 3¼ miles (5.2km)

**TIME** 2 hours

**PARKING** Car park at start

**ROUTE FEATURES** Grassy tracks; steep paths; spectacular cliff scenery; views; industrial history

**GPS WAYPOINTS**
- SO 208 154
- Ⓐ SO 200 159
- Ⓑ SO 198 161
- Ⓒ SO 188 160
- Ⓓ SO 197 159
- Ⓔ SO 205 154

**PUBLIC TRANSPORT** None

**REFRESHMENTS** None

**PUBLIC TOILETS** None

**PLAY AREA** None

**ORDNANCE SURVEY MAPS** Explorer OL13 (Brecon Beacons National Park – Eastern area), Landranger 161 (The Black Mountains)

Walk out of the car park and back down the access track to the road. Turn left and follow this along to some cottages on your left. Keep straight ahead as the road veers round to the right, and continue past the final cottage and out onto the open hillside on a broad grassy track that was once a tram road used for carrying limestone from the quarries above. Continue easily along until some large blocks of limestone partly block the path. Look to the right and you'll make out the remains of a built-up platform Ⓐ.

Turn right here and descend steeply to the corner of the wood below Ⓑ. Here you'll see the remains of an old wheelman's hut and also a park bench, that offers fine views over the Usk Valley. Turn left here onto a narrow but clear path that is often covered by bracken in the summer. Follow it uphill slightly at first and then contour around the hillside, with great views ahead to the imposing cliffs of Craig y Cilau. The path then drops to the banks of a small stream that emerges from a wall on the floor of the valley.

> **?** *What's wrong with the name of the cottage near the start of the walk?*

Turn left and keep the wall to your right to walk along a rough path that passes a Nature Reserve sign and climbs steadily upwards.

*Limestone cliffs near Craig y Cilau*

Continue for nearly ½ mile, and then as you divert to the left to pass the very obvious corner of a wall, you'll see a waymark post pointing you straight ahead. Continue for another few paces with the wall to your right, and you'll meet another waymark post – this one diverting you sharp left onto a narrow path **C**.

The path is narrow and reasonably level to start with but it soon steepens and climbs stiffly to a grassy bank with a marker post on it. Keep ahead to continue upwards until you eventually reach a good level track. This is another of the old tram roads that was used to transport the limestone from the quarries. To your right, 300 yds farther on, is Ogof Agen Allwedd, the entrance to one of the longest cave systems in Britain. You turn left however, and follow the easy track eastwards past a sign for the nature reserve. Continue for 100 yds beyond this and then fork right on to an obvious but narrow path that leads up onto a plateau dotted with small piles of spoil **D**.

Follow the narrow path as it undulates along with the cliffs uphill to your right. Keep right at any forks and eventually you'll find yourself

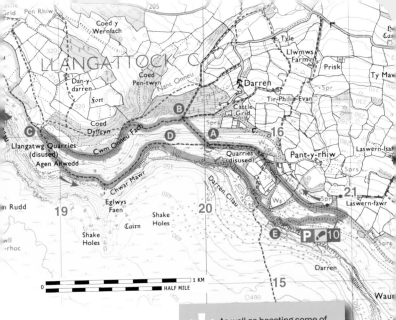

on a clearer, broader track that heads leftwards around the huge banks of spoil at Chwar Pant-y-Rhiw. Continue until a good track joins from the right. This comes through the cutting between the banks and the quarry faces. Now, at the next fork, bear left, to follow a good firm track downwards to a junction of tracks **E**. A brief detour to the right will expose a lime-kiln and tumbledown quarry building. Keep ahead, still on a good track and this will drop you back easily to the car park. ∎

⁎ As well as boasting some of the best views in the whole National Park, the **Llangattock Escarpment** conceals some wonderful **industrial history**. The limestone escarpment was quarried from the early 19th-century, if not earlier, and the tracks that this walk follows were once all part of the sophisticated transport network used to get the quarried stone and lime down to the Monmouthshire and Brecon Canal, near Llangattock village. The building at the top of the steep path at **A** was once a wheelhouse and the steep path, an incline down which the stone was lowered. The flat, broad tramways now make wonderful footpaths and the grass-covered spoil heaps only add to the overall atmosphere.

# The Blorenge

- Wonderful views
- grouse moor
- hang-gliders
- famous grave

*The imposing bulk of the Blorenge towers above Abergavenny offering surprisingly easy walking as well as wonderful views across the small town to the sprawling massif of the Black Mountains. This walk uses broad, easy-to-follow tracks to explore the mountain's impressive north-facing escarpment and to cross its austere summit plateau. Take a picnic.*

The Blorenge

# walk 11

**START** Carn-y-gorfydd
Roadside Rest

**DISTANCE** 3½ miles (5.6km)

**TIME** 2 hours

**PARKING** Car park at start

**ROUTE FEATURES** Grassy
tracks; muddy paths;
views; rocky summit;
quiet road section

**GPS WAYPOINTS**
SO 270 109
Ⓐ SO 277 122
Ⓑ SO 270 118
Ⓒ SO 263 107

**PUBLIC TRANSPORT** None

**REFRESHMENTS** None

**PUBLIC TOILETS** None

**PLAY AREA** None

**ORDNANCE SURVEY MAPS**
Explorer OL13 (Brecon
Beacons National
Park – Eastern area),
Landranger 161 (The
Black Mountains)

Leave the car park and follow the narrow lane downhill for 500 yds to a grassy track on the left, guarded by a green-painted barrier. Go around this and follow the track steeply uphill with the views over the Usk Valley opening up all the time as you go. Stay with it all the way to the top, passing some grassy banks created by quarrying spoil, until you reach a small brick hut Ⓐ that marks the start of the path up towards the summit. For now though, continue around the escarpment edge, with the drop into the valley to your right. This offers some wonderful views across Abergavenny to the Sugar Loaf and also to the Black Mountains, farther west. Continue around the escarpment as far as you wish. The small rocky outcrops that crown the steep hillside provide plenty of shelter so the grassy terraces between make perfect, very scenic picnic spots.

This mountain is very popular with hang-gliders and paragliders, who make the most of the up-draughts to fly out above the Usk Valley. It is actually owned by the South East Wales Hang Gliding & Paragliding Club.

When you've finished your exploration, return to the small brick hut, and turn right, to follow a rough track up the hill above it. Cross a short boggy patch and then climb a short steep stretch that gives you access to the true summit plateau. This was once the most southerly of Britain's managed grouse moors and you are still very likely to see or even hear red grouse as you walk along this section; listen out for their disgruntled calls that at times actually sound as if they are saying 'get back, get back!'

Continue along the main track to the rocky top; crowned with a whitewashed trig point **B**. The summit was once marked with an ancient burial cairn, which is where all the stones come from. From here, keep heading in the same direction, now aiming towards the two huge masts that you can see on the horizon. Shortly before you reach the masts, you'll see a car park ahead. Approximately 50 yds before you reach this, you'll see a faint grassy track that leads off diagonally right, towards a seat. Follow

Britain won just one gold medal in the 1952 Olympic Games, held in Helsinki, and that was in the show jumping, where Welshman Sir Harry Llewellyn rode a beautiful horse named Foxhunter to a famous victory. They were an invincible pairing; winning 78 international trophies together during the 1950s. After his death, in 1959, Foxhunter was buried on top of the Blorenge, where you'll see a small memorial plaque. Sir Harry, who was born in Aberdare but actually lived near Abergavenny, died after a long illness in 1999, aged 88. His ashes were scattered by the grave of his famous mount.

*Quarried limestone, the Blorenge*

this and then clamber over the small bank to find the grave of *Foxhunter*, a famous horse which was buried here **C**.

**? How old was Foxhunter when he died?**

Now follow the path out to the car park and masts, where you need to turn left to walk down the narrow lane to the car park. ■

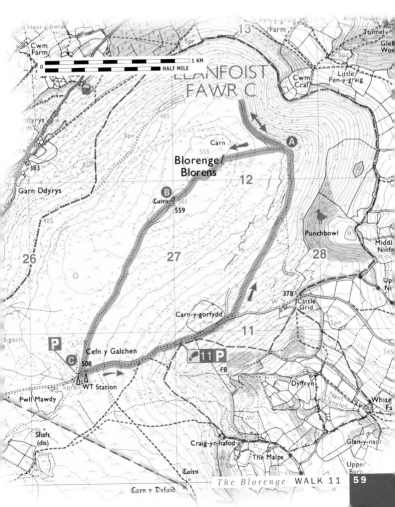

# Craig Cerrig-gleisiad

- Nature reserve
- glacial landscape
- craggy cliffs
- Alpine flora

*walk 12*

*This walk is two walks in one. The longer outing climbs above the dramatic escarpment of Craig Cerrig-gleisiad on easy-to-follow paths that are steep in places. The shorter walk takes an easy trail into the very heart of the National Nature Reserve and offers a chance to see the geological effects of the receding Ice Ages as well as the unique flora and fauna left behind.*

*Craig Cerrig-gleisiad in snow*

# walk 12

**START** Craig Cerrig-gleisiad picnic area

**DISTANCE** 4 miles (6.4km) or 1¼ miles (1.9km)

**TIME** 2 hours or 1 hour

**PARKING** At the picnic area. No charge

**ROUTE FEATURES** Rocky escarpment and cliffs; steep climb; clear tracks; muddy paths; stream crossings. Shorter route: rocky escarpment and cliffs; muddy paths; some stiles

**GPS WAYPOINTS**
🖉 SN 971 222
Ⓐ SN 969 221
Ⓑ SN 966 236
Ⓒ SN 958 227
Ⓓ SN 959 225
Ⓔ SN 961 222

**PUBLIC TRANSPORT** Buses between Brecon and Merthyr Tydfil, also summer Beacons Bus services

**REFRESHMENTS** None

**PUBLIC TOILETS** 2 miles south in Forest car park

**PLAY AREA** None

**ORDNANCE SURVEY MAPS** Explorer OL12 (Brecon Beacons National Park – Western & Central areas), Landranger 160 (Brecon Beacons)

🖉 From the lay-by, go through the kissing-gate and follow the footpath up the valley for 300 yds to a dry stone wall Ⓐ. Go through a gap in the wall and turn right to follow the clear path around the hillside with the wall to your right. Drop to cross a small brook and climb slightly to continue in the same direction with great views over the Tarell Valley to the high mountains of the Brecon Beacons on the other side of the A470. Cross another brook and climb back up again. Now continue until you reach a kissing-gate that leads onto a clear track, with fine views to the north Ⓑ.

> **?** *How many different flowers and birds can you spot?*

Turn left and climb steeply up the hill, all the time staying on the clear main track. Eventually you'll come to a gate and a stile, that give access to open ground beyond. Continue along the track until a clear turning to the right leads you to the trig point that marks the summit of Fan Frynych Ⓒ.

Facing back the way that you came, you'll see two tracks leading away from the trig point. Take the right-hand one and ignore a fork to the right almost immediately. Continue to another fork and bear right to drop back onto the main track.

Ⓓ Turn right onto this and follow the fence along until you come to a kissing-gate on

*Looking up to Craig Cerrig Gleisiad from near the start*

your left, marked with Beacons Way signs. Go through this and follow the path around the hillside, ignoring a right fork, until you reach a junction with another path in an obvious shallow groove. Bear right here to follow a line of fence posts steeply down. This leads onto some grassy moraine banks at the foot of the steep cliffs in the very heart of the nature reserve **E**.

Bear around to the left to follow the path across the banks and down to the banks of a stream, where you'll soon arrive at the gate you passed through on the way out. Keep ahead to retrace your earlier footsteps back to the car park.

*For the shorter route, from **A**, keep straight ahead and walk in towards the foot of*

The **north-facing cliffs** of Craig Cerrig-gleisiad – which translates to Blue-stone Rock – were **formed** by glacial action **during the last Ice Age**. The ice scoured out the deep hollow in the hillside, that you see today, before depositing the rocks it picked up into large banks known as 'moraine'. Amazingly, the cool conditions created by the constant shade of the north-facing cliffs, have enabled a selection of arctic – alpine plants to continue to flourish. These plants, which include saxifrages and roseroot, thrive on the lime-rich soil around the cliffs. The diversity of the National Nature Reserve stretches beyond flora with 16 different species of butterfly and over 80 species of bird observed here too.

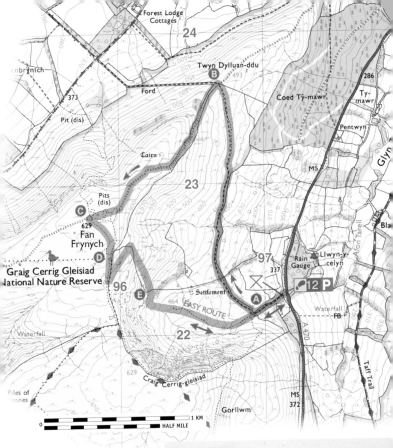

the cliffs **E**. You can walk to the very base of the steeper ground if you wish. The area here makes for interesting exploration so take your time and enjoy the unusual nature and magnificent scenery. Return by the same route.

*Craig Cerrig-gleisiad from Fan Fawr*

# Grwyne Fawr Reservoir

- Huge reservoir dam
- mountain tracks
- look out for dippers
- lovely picnic spot

*walk 13*

The Grwyne Fawr Valley runs all the way from the highest ground in the Black Mountains to the village of Glangrwyney, near Abergavenny, where it finally empties into the Usk. The hillsides that form the head of the valley cradle a sizeable reservoir that makes a fine objective for a walk. This is a lengthy but easy expedition ending with a beautiful riverside stroll.

The Grwyne Fawr Reservoir

| | |
|---|---|
| **START** | Mynydd Du Forest |
| **DISTANCE** | 4 miles (6.4km) |
| **TIME** | 2 hours |
| **PARKING** | At the start |
| **ROUTE FEATURES** | Clear rocky paths; grassy meadows; open moorland; reservoir; riverside road; picnic areas |

**GPS WAYPOINTS**

🖊 SO 252 284
Ⓐ SO 248 292
Ⓑ SO 233 308
Ⓒ SO 234 306

| | |
|---|---|
| **PUBLIC TRANSPORT** | None |
| **REFRESHMENTS** | None |
| **PUBLIC TOILETS** | None |
| **PLAY AREA** | None |

**ORDNANCE SURVEY MAPS**
Explorer OL13 (Brecon Beacons National Park – Eastern area), Landranger 161 (The Black Mountains)

🥾 Head out of the far end of the car park and turn right onto the road. After just a few paces, bear right onto a steep stony track and climb up with the wood to your right and the valley floor below you to the left. The woodland is a great place to spot different fungi; especially in autumn and early winter. Continue up keeping left at a fork with a bridleway, and eventually leaving the woods behind Ⓐ. Now keep ahead with great views

> ✳ The **Grwyne Fawr Reservoir** was once the highest reservoir in the whole of Britain, with the upper water level reaching an impressive 1,935ft (590m) above sea level. Work began on the dam as early as 1912 but the hostilities of the First World War delayed the proceedings and it wasn't completed until 1928. The dam spans some 327m and the walls at its base are over 40m thick. When full the reservoir can hold around 370 million gallons of water, which is then carried to towns as far away as Abertillery by a network of underground pipes. The reservoir's biggest claim to fame was when Prince Harry was photographed abseiling down the dam wall as part of an adventure weekend in 1998.

over the ever deepening valley down to your left. The steep hillside on the other side of the valley forms the lower flanks of the Gadair Ridge and is topped with Waun Fach and Pen y Gadair Fawr, the two highest peaks in the Black Mountains.

Grwyne Fawr, Brecon Beacons

Continue through a succession of gates until the track eventually levels and you see a stand of conifers ahead. This marks the reservoir grounds. Continue until you reach the grounds and go through the gate on your left to gain access to the huge dam **B**. Walk across the dam and then, when you get to the other side, turn left to climb a steep bank dotted with a few trees. Continue in the same direction until you reach the far side of the bank, where you'll see a clearer path leading down to a fence.

**?** *How wide do you think the dam wall is at the top — on the part that you walk over?*

Drop to the fence and bear left to follow it down to a stile. Cross this and drop down the steep hillside on a faint zigzag path that eventually leads out onto a narrow tarmac lane **C**, which is the dam access road. Turn right onto this and continue easily along it with the Grwyne Fawr River on your left. There are numerous rapids and cascades all the way down and this is a great spot to see dippers; small black and white birds that feed on aquatic larvae by actually walking beneath the fast flowing water. Herons also ply their trade on the banks of the river.

Grwyne Fawr Reservoir

Rain Gauge

**B**

Weirs

FB

Sheepfolds

FB

**C**

Y Fan

Cairns

Blacksmith's Anvil (Stone)

Cairns

30

1 KM

HALF MILE

Nant Yr Helyg

Sheepfold

24

25

Grwyne Fawr

**A**

3

29

Waterfall

Pen y Gadair Fawr

**The Black Mountains/ Y Mynyddoedd Duon**

**P** 🖊 **13**

378

Blaen-y-cwm

**i**

**!**

Follow the road down, bridging the river after a short distance, and then passing beneath an isolated cottage. Eventually the road veers away but the walk continues along it, now with a lovely grassy area to your left from the riverbanks. This is a fine picnic spot but be warned; it gets very busy in the summer. Keep as close to the banks as you can and continue easily downstream until you pass the track you followed on the way out. Continue for a few paces and then turn left, back into the car park. ■

The huge dam of the Grwyne Fawr Reservoir

# Goytre Wharf and Pentre Hill

- ■ **Woodland trails**
- ■ **canal towpath**
- ■ **country inn**
- ■ **pleasure boats**

*Goytre Wharf is the undisputed highlight of a narrow finger of land that defines the south east corner of the National Park. This is an enjoyable ramble, which starts and finishes on the waterside, but climbs steeply up into the surrounding woodland. A short detour can be made to an excellent, tucked-away, country inn; or there's a great restaurant back at the canal side.*

walk 14

Monmouthshire and Brecon Canal near Goytre

# *walk* **14**

**START** Goytre Wharf

**DISTANCE** 4½ miles (7.2km)

**TIME** 2 hours

**PARKING** Pay and Display at the start

**ROUTE FEATURES**
Woodland trails; muddy field paths; meadows; canal towpath

**GPS WAYPOINTS**
🖉 SO 311 064
Ⓐ SO 305 064
Ⓑ SO 302 069
Ⓒ SO 297 071
Ⓓ SO 296 076
Ⓔ SO 300 075
Ⓕ SO 309 077

**PUBLIC TRANSPORT** Buses between Abergavenny and Goytre village

**REFRESHMENTS**
Restaurant at the start and the Goose and Cuckoo public house a few minutes from the walk

**PUBLIC TOILETS** At start

**PLAY AREA** At start

**ORDNANCE SURVEY MAPS**
Explorer OL13 (Brecon Beacons National Park – Eastern area), Landranger 161 (The Black Mountains)

From the car park, head back out of the drive to the road and turn left. Immediately turn right, over a stile, and walk up through the field to another stile. Keep ahead to

> ✱ Originally known as the Breckneck and Abergavenny Canal, the 33-mile long **Monmouthshire and Brecon Canal** was constructed between 1797 and 1812, to link Brecon with the Bristol Channel port of Newport. It was mainly used to carry stone and processed lime from local quarries but these days it sees only leisure traffic.

another stile and cross this to another stile, which you also cross, now with the hedge to your right. Keep ahead to another stile at the foot of some woodland Ⓐ. Cross the stile and turn right, to walk along a broad forest track that skirts the bottom of the woodland. Ignore a track leading up into the wood and continue around until you reach a junction with another track that drops down to your right. If you miss it, you'll soon come to a gate that blocks your way. Drop down to the road Ⓑ.

Now cross the road to walk up the narrow lane opposite. Continue past a drive on the right, that leads to a large house, and you'll soon come to the corner of a wood on your right; with footpaths going both right and left. Take the left one, and climb steeply up the edge of a field and through a gap to continue up the edge of the next field. At the top of this one, bear right to walk around the top of the field to a gateway on the left. Go through this and turn right to keep to the right-hand edge of the next field. Turn left in the corner and walk up, with the hedge to your right, to a stile beneath a house 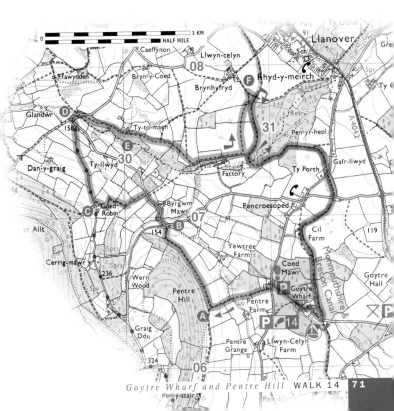.

> **?** *Which trees that you see on the walk will produce acorns?*

Do not cross the stile but instead turn right ahead of it, to keep the hedge and house to your left as you walk along the top of a field to a stile that leads onto a sunken track. Turn right onto this track and follow it all the way down to the road **D**. Turn left and immediately right, to drop down to a bridge. *For the Goose and Cuckoo, ignore the right*

*Canal boat near Goytre Wharf*

*turn and continue uphill.* Cross the bridge before turning right onto a waymarked footpath. The path is vague at this point but keep ahead for approximately 10 yds and then bear left to climb steeply up a bank to join a good drive at the top. Bear right onto this and follow it past a house, keeping the house to your left **E**.

Now keep straight ahead until you reach a wood. Go over the stile and turn right and then left to keep straight ahead with a pond to your right. Continue to a stile that leads back onto open pasture and bear half right to drop to the right-hand hedge. Now follow the field edge down to a gap, where you keep straight ahead again, to walk along with the hedge now to your right. Continue until you are almost back on the canal, where a waymark post directs you left, across the field to a gate. Go through this and cross the next field to a gate that leads onto a track. Turn right onto this to cross the canal on a bridge **F**. Drop down to join the towpath and follow it all the way back to Goytre Wharf. Here, you bear left to drop down from the towpath and then turn right to walk beneath the aqueduct back to the car park.

■

# The Taf Fechan Forest

- ◼ Upland reservoir
- ◼ enchanting riverside
- ◼ forest trails
- ◼ fine views

*Delightfully easy walking around a picturesque valley that cuts deeply into the southern slopes of the National Park's highest mountains. This walk has a little of everything from broad forest tracks, with fine views, to a secret winding riverside path that feels almost enchanted. Some sections can be wet and muddy so good boots will be an advantage.*

*walk 15*

Afon Taf Fechan, Taf Fechan Forest

# walk 15

**START** Owl's Grove recreation area

**DISTANCE** 4 miles (6.4km)

**TIME** 2 hours

**PARKING** At the start

**ROUTE FEATURES** Woodland; riverside paths; boggy moorland

**GPS WAYPOINTS**
- SO 048 162
- Ⓐ SO 049 167
- Ⓑ SO 035 173
- Ⓒ SO 033 181
- Ⓓ SO 031 179
- Ⓔ SO 028 180
- Ⓕ SO 042 161

**PUBLIC TRANSPORT** Summer bus service from Brecon and Talybont-on-Usk

**REFRESHMENTS** None

**PUBLIC TOILETS** None

**PLAY AREA** At start

**ORDNANCE SURVEY MAPS** Explorer OL12 (Brecon Beacons National Park – Western & Central areas), Landranger 160 (Brecon Beacons)

Walk out onto the road and turn right to walk steeply uphill for a few minutes. As you reach the top, bear left onto a broad forest track Ⓐ and then, after just a few paces, keep straight ahead at a fork, with another track dropping to your left. Continue along here for ½ mile or so and keep left at a fork, through a gate, to continue easily, with fine views over the valley below, to a junction with a narrow lane Ⓑ.

Turn right onto the lane and then turn straightaway right again, onto a broad muddy track that climbs up the edge of the forest. Follow this uphill, now with excellent views across the head of the Taf Fechan Valley, until you reach a gate above a deep, steep-sided ravine. Continue down into the ravine and ford the stream at the bottom before climbing steeply out again. At the top, bear left onto a grassy track Ⓒ with wonderful views up to Pen y Fan and Cribyn. Follow this down to a gate and go through before turning left onto a track. Follow this for a few paces and when you meet a fence turn right to drop down a muddy path to the main entrance of the reservoir grounds Ⓓ.

Do not go through but instead turn right and then bear slightly left to pick up a clear path. Drop down into a dip and cross a concrete bridge over the reservoir outfall before climbing steeply up onto the grassy top of the dam. Bear left here to follow this along, with great views up the valley to Pen y Fan

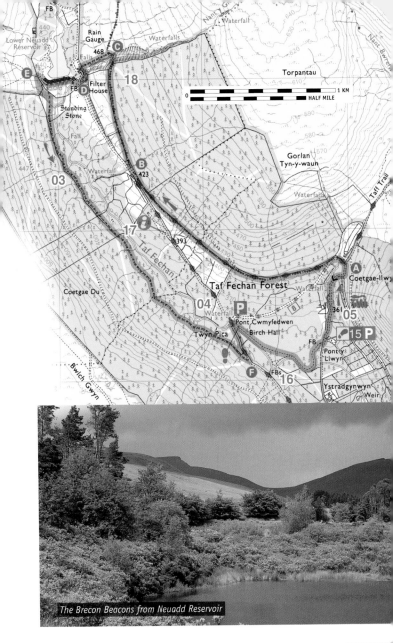

The Brecon Beacons from Neuadd Reservoir

*Pen y Fan from the Neuadd Reservoir*

and Corn Du, the highest mountains in the National Park, and then keep straight ahead to go through a gate and out onto open moorland **E**.

> ✳ The **two Neuadd reservoirs** passed on the walk were constructed to supply water to Merthyr Tydfil during its heyday as a boomtown in the industrial revolution. The lower one was opened in 1884 but demand soon outstripped supply and the river was flooded again, higher up the valley.

Bear left to follow a faint path downhill (waymark on post). Merge with another path and keep ahead right to drop down over a brook. Now aim for the stile that you see ahead and this marks the start of a clear but often boggy and muddy path that heads down the valley with the forest to your right and the Taf Fechan River down to your left. The path gradually improves to become a well-surfaced forest track after

½ mile or so. Stay with it, keeping ahead the whole time, and eventually you'll meet the road **F**.

**?** *Which is the tallest of the three mountains that you can see at the head of the valley?*

Turn left onto the road and walk uphill to a bridge with spectacular waterfalls to your left. Cross the bridge and turn right, as if entering the car park, and then turn right again, to follow a good path into the woods with the river to your right. Follow this easily along, passing a wooden footbridge to the right after a few paces. Continue along the bank until, after approximately ½ mile, the path veers left away from the river, now following the bank of a smaller tributary. Continue easily upstream to a small footbridge on the right. Cross this and you'll see the car park straight ahead.

# The Waterfalls Walk

- Spectacular falls
- river birdlife
- walk beneath fall
- enormous cave

*The Ystradfellte waterfalls are one of the real jewels in the Brecon Beacons crown; especially when the cloud comes down, obscuring the views from the hilltops. This is a longish walk, and there are a few very steep stepped sections to negotiate. The rewards are wonderful with some breathtaking scenery in places. Take waterproofs if you wish to walk behind the falls.*

Sgwd yr Pannwr

| | |
|---|---|
| **START** Porth yr Ogof car park | |
| **DISTANCE** 5 miles (8km) | |
| **TIME** 2 hours | |
| **PARKING** Supervised fee-paying car park at the start | |
| **ROUTE FEATURES** Slippery rock; roots; steep steps; muddy tracks; forest trails; waterfalls | |

**GPS WAYPOINTS**

- 📷 SN 928 124
- Ⓐ SN 927 124
- Ⓑ SN 924 111
- Ⓒ SN 926 110
- Ⓓ SN 927 100
- Ⓔ SN 926 101
- Ⓕ SN 922 103
- Ⓖ SN 923 106
- Ⓗ SN 924 109

**PUBLIC TRANSPORT** None

**REFRESHMENTS** None

**PUBLIC TOILETS** At the start

**PLAY AREA** At the start

**ORDNANCE SURVEY MAPS** Explorer OL12 (Brecon Beacons National Park – Western & Central areas), Landranger 160 (Brecon Beacons)

📷 Before heading off for the waterfalls, it's well worth visiting Porth yr Ogof, one of the largest cave entrances in Wales, which is situated just a few metres below the car park. Descend the steps that lead from the bottom of the car park, beneath the toilet block, and then turn left at the bottom to walk along the rocky bank to the gargantuan mouth of the cave. *It's possible to walk a short way in but great care is needed, as the rock can be very slippery and the river is very powerful and dangerous.*

Walk back up towards the car park and bear right to walk out to the road Ⓐ.

Go straight across and take the left-hand of the two paths, waymarked with a yellow arrow. Pass a right turn (cavers only) and follow the main path through a kissing-gate and down to the grassy riverbank. Bear left here and follow the Afon Mellte downstream. *The path is easy in some places but awkward*

> ✳ The **geology** of this area is fairly complex with layers of carboniferous limestone interspersed with layers of much harder old red sandstone as well as considerably softer shales. The **waterfalls** have been formed where layers of the harder rock have created shelves that cannot be worn down by the fast flowing rivers. As soon as the water passes downstream of these shelves, it continues the erosion process, creating a steep drop.

*in others. Take care crossing the steeper sections and remember that the rocks and roots can be slippery.* Like many of the rivers in the area, this is a good place to see dippers and some of the slower moving pools are also home to kingfishers. Eventually you'll come to a footbridge that spans the river **B**.

There are three big waterfalls on this walk but how many smaller ones can you count?

Do not cross the bridge, instead keep ahead to drop into a dip and climb steeply out again. Continue up to a fence on your left and then, where

Sgwd Isaf Clun Gwyn, Ystradfellte

you see a wooden fence ahead and to the right, climb up a few more feet to a junction of tracks marked with a large fingerpost. Bear left onto the well-surfaced path, signed to Gwaun Hepste, and follow this to a crossroads of tracks **C**.

Bear right here, which is signposted Sgwd yr Eira, and follow the red-topped waymarks along the forest track. Stay with this for a while now, ducking into a particularly dark section of woodland before it opens out into mixed woodland again. Continue until a waymark post directs you right, downhill. Drop down a few steps and continue down until you join into an open track, that runs along the edge of the steep gorge ahead **D**.

Turn right onto this, for a few paces and then turn left to drop steeply down a series of steps to the magnificent waterfall of Sgwyd yr Eira. Turn left to walk carefully along the bank and behind the falls – *this can be slippery and if the falls are very full you are likely to get wet*. Then retrace your steps all the way back to the top of the steps and turn left to continue around the hillside. Pass a seat to your left – a fine viewpoint – and continue until you reach a green waymark directing you downhill to the left **E**. Follow this down and keep left at a fork. This will lead you to Sgwd y Pannwr (the Falls of the Fuller) **F**. Now follow the Afon Mellte upstream past a number of pools to the next waterfall,

Beneath the falls at Sgwd yr Eira

which is Sgwd Isaf Clun-Gwyn (the Lower Falls of the White Meadow) . For the best views, scramble up the bank for a few metres.

Now retrace your steps back downstream and bear left at the first opportunity to climb back up to the fork you visited earlier. Keep ahead to climb back up to the top path again . Bear left onto this and follow it for some distance now, until you see a wooden fence down to your left. This marks the viewing position above the final waterfall, Sgwd Uchaf Clun-Gwyn (the Upper Falls of the White Meadow) . Drop to the left for the viewing area.

Climb back up to the path above and turn left to follow the fence along to meet the path that you walked along earlier. Keep left to follow this down to the footbridge you passed on the way out and keep ahead to follow the Afon Mellte back upstream. The grassy bank near the car park makes a great place to while away the rest of the afternoon if you've time to spare.

# The Sugar Loaf

- Mountain scenery
- rocky summit
- incredible views
- mountain birdlife

*This is one of the toughest walks in the book but still perfectly achievable if taken slowly and steadily. The Sugar Loaf stands aloof from the Black Mountains but offers wonderful views across them, as well as over the Usk Valley and the town of Abergavenny. Meadow pipits, skylarks and even the occasional grouse live on the heathery slopes, and ravens frequent the rocky tops.*

*walk 17*

Sugar Loaf summit

# walk 17

**START** Mynydd Llanwenarth viewpoint

**DISTANCE** 4½ miles (7.2km)

**TIME** 3 hours

**PARKING** At the start

**ROUTE FEATURES** Grassy mountain paths; rocky summit

**GPS WAYPOINTS**
🖉 SO 268 167
Ⓐ SO 267 172
Ⓑ SO 260 183
Ⓒ SO 255 182
Ⓓ SO 272 187

**PUBLIC TRANSPORT** None

**REFRESHMENTS** None

**PUBLIC TOILETS** None

**PLAY AREA** None

**ORDNANCE SURVEY MAPS**
Explorer OL13 (Brecon Beacons National Park – Eastern area), Landranger 161 (The Black Mountains)

🖉 Standing in the car park and looking up the slope, there are three obvious tracks leading away.

The lowest, to your left, is a tarmac drive. The highest goes straight uphill past a National Trust sign. Between these, running diagonally half-left is a broad grassy track, dotted with a few rocks. Take this and follow it upwards to the corner of a dry stone wall Ⓐ. Keep straight ahead, with the wall to your left, and ignore any tracks that lead off to the right.

Eventually, you'll start to drop into a deep valley, where the path finally veers away from the wall and drops diagonally across the hillside towards the far corner of a wood. Upon reaching the corner of the wood, turn left to descend a steep grassy path to the stream Ⓑ. Keep ahead to climb away from the stream, and follow the obvious main path steeply uphill and onto a distinct shoulder, with a steep slope to your right and a wall to your left. Continue until the path reaches the crest and then, with the corner of the wall and a gate directly ahead of you Ⓒ, turn right to cross some rough ground. You will locate a good path that climbs up the centre of the grassy ridge with good views in both directions.

As the track levels, you'll be joined by another track coming in from the left. Ignore this and continue straight ahead to climb steeply up the narrowing ridge. This is a great place

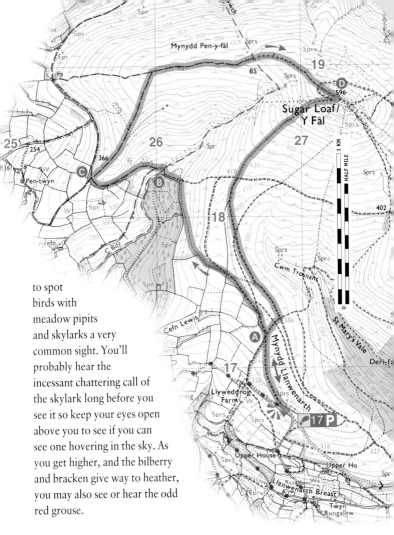

to spot birds with meadow pipits and skylarks a very common sight. You'll probably hear the incessant chattering call of the skylark long before you see it so keep your eyes open above you to see if you can see one hovering in the sky. As you get higher, and the bilberry and bracken give way to heather, you may also see or hear the odd red grouse.

A final steep section gives access to jumbled rocks that mark the western end of the summit. The rocks offer wonderful views west, across the Grwyne Fawr Valley to the Black Mountains. Continue straight ahead, on a narrow path that weaves between the rocks, and you'll soon come to the whitewashed trig point **D**.

It's a good idea to take a few moments to gain your bearings here. Look back down towards the car park, which you cannot actually see from the summit, and you'll notice that there are a lot of different tracks that cross the hillside; many of them not shown on the map. The valley down to your left is St Mary's Vale (see Walk 3). The descent route contours around the head of this valley rather than dropping into it.

Follow the narrow path that leads downhill to the right

The Sugar Loaf, or Mynydd Pen-y-fâl, to give it its true Welsh name, is one of the most distinctive and popular peaks in the National Park. Its rugged cone-shaped summit can be seen from many miles around and its bracken-covered slopes are criss-crossed with a good network of grassy paths that make it one of the easier peaks to climb. It's quite distinct from the Black Mountains, which sit on the other side of the gaping chasm of the Grwyne Fawr Valley (see Walk 13), and is usually classified as one of the three Abergavenny Peaks, along with Ysgyryd Fawr and the Blorenge (see Walk 11).

*The Sugar loaf from the west*

Looking towards the Sugar Loaf from Abergavenny

from the trig point and
continue steeply down until
you reach the level ground
that marks the head of St
Mary's Vale. Circle around
the valley and continue
along the main track, with the

**?** *Can you recognise the other two Abergavenny mountains of the Blorenge and Ysgyryd Fawr?*

valley now to your left and the crest of the ridge to your right, until you
reach a broad grassy square that is actually a fairly major crossroads of
tracks. Turn right here to cross the crest of the ridge and you should be
able to see a wall ahead – this is the wall that you followed on the way
out. Continue until you reach it and then bear left to retrace your earlier
footsteps back to the car park.  ■

# The Cat's Back and Black Hill

■ Rocky ridge
■ mountain scenery

■ great views
■ deep valley

*A pedigree mountain walk that should not prove too much of a challenge as long as it's taken slowly and the weather stays fine. The rewards for the effort are tremendous; with an airy traverse of one of the Black Mountain's finest ridges and some stunning views over the Hereford countryside to the Malvern Hills.*

*walk 18*

*The Black Mountains from the Cat's Back*

**START** Black Hill picnic area

**DISTANCE** 5 miles (8km)

**TIME** 3 hours

**PARKING** At the start

**ROUTE FEATURES** Rocky ridge; open moorland; steep valley path; narrow lane

**GPS WAYPOINTS**
🖉 SO 288 328
Ⓐ SO 284 332
Ⓑ SO 274 348
Ⓒ SO 263 353
Ⓓ SO 273 337

**PUBLIC TRANSPORT** None suitable

**REFRESHMENTS** None

**PUBLIC TOILETS** None

**PLAY AREA** At the start

**ORDNANCE SURVEY MAPS** Explorer OL13 (Brecon Beacons National Park – Eastern area), Landranger 161 (The Black Mountains)

🖉 Leave the car park and picnic tables and head uphill towards the obvious hillside. Cross the rickety old stile (or go through the gate) to gain access to the open hillside. The main track bears away to the right to contour around the hillside so leave it to the left and climb steeply up the centre of the obvious sharp prow. This is the steepest section of the walk and, in fact, one of the steepest paths in the whole book. It's not very long though, so take your time and you'll soon be cresting the rise at the southern end of a wonderful narrow ridge Ⓐ.

**?** This walk is very close to the border of England and Wales. Which country is Herefordshire part of?

Once up, keep ahead to follow the airy skyline walkway easily northwards over numerous short and craggy steps. The views to the east, over the flat lands of the Herefordshire countryside, are wonderful. So are those to the west, across the magnificent Olchon Valley to the Hatterrall Ridge, which actually defines the border between England and Wales as well as forming the eastern boundary of the National Park. You'll also notice some spectacular thorn trees growing out of the near vertical valley sides.

Eventually the spur starts to broaden and you'll start the final easy ascent to Black Hill's

The highest ground in England is actually Scafell Pike in the Lake District, which is 3,205ft (977m) above sea level. There is often debate about which is the highest ground in southern England, an accolade often incorrectly handed to High Willhays on Dartmoor, which is actually only 2,037ft (621m) above sea level as opposed to the **highest point of the Hatterrall Ridge**, very close to this walk, which is **2,306ft (703m)**. Even Black Hill, which is actually visited on this walk, is notably higher than any of the ground on Dartmoor or Derbyshire's Peak District.

The Cat's Back, Black Hill

2,100ft trig point **B**, which you'll see protruding sharply from the heather and bilberry. Once there, fork left to follow a faint path away from the summit, keeping the small pool to your right. Continue easily downwards for approximately 15 minutes, and then in the bottom of the dip, you'll see a small cairn that marks a barely discernable junction of paths **C**. Turn left here, onto a very faint grassy track, and follow it down into an obvious notch that quickly deepens to become the head of the spectacular Olchon Valley.

Stay with the path as it becomes more established; dropping down the side of a small brook and eventually developing into a broad and rocky track that dips steeply down the head of the valley, where you'll see some small waterfalls decorating

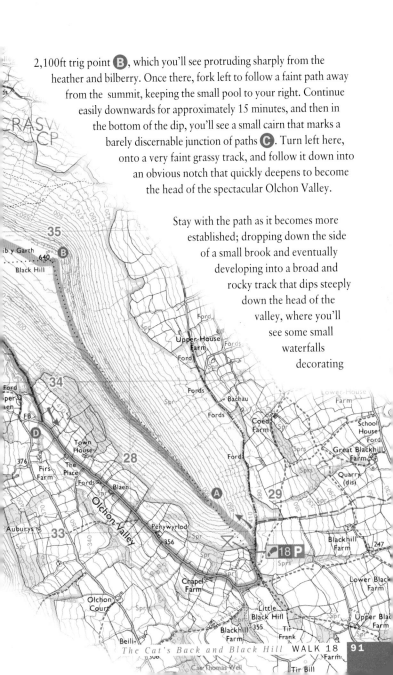

The summit of Black Hill

the Olchon Brook to your right and some lofty crags crowning the steep hillside opposite. Continue steeply down until the going eases and the path flattens out nicely to make a pleasant and gentle walk, a few metres above the infant river.

Continue over a couple of small tributaries to a gate in a corner that leads in turn onto a sunken green lane. Follow this easily down until it merges with a narrow tarmac road **D**. Bear left onto this lane and follow it for just over one mile to a T-junction. Turn left here and climb steeply back up to the car park on the same lane that you drove in on earlier.

# The Usk Reservoir

- Woodland trails
- lakeside paths
- lovely views
- easy walking

*This is the longest walk in the book but it follows good trails and is therefore reasonably easy-going. The reservoir itself is a hidden gem. Concealed by dense woodland and surrounded by some very remote moorland it offers great views over the surrounding countryside and is also a good place to spot wildlife, particularly waterfowl and red kites.*

Usk Reservoir

# walk 19

**START** Car park and picnic area near Pont'ar Wysg

**DISTANCE** 5$\frac{1}{2}$ miles (8.8km)

**TIME** 2$\frac{1}{2}$ hours

**PARKING** At the start

**ROUTE FEATURES** Forest tracks; lakeside paths; tarmac lane

**GPS WAYPOINTS**
- SN 819 271
- **A** SN 817 275
- **B** SN 805 278
- **C** SN 816 284
- **D** SN 825 293
- **E** SN 827 279

**PUBLIC TRANSPORT** None

**REFRESHMENTS** None

**PUBLIC TOILETS** None

**PLAY AREA** None

**ORDNANCE SURVEY MAPS** Explorer OL12 (Brecon Beacons National Park – Western & Central areas), Landranger 160 (Brecon Beacons)

From the car park, walk back out onto the road and cross it to go through a gate onto a path. You'll see the bicycle trail waymark disc on the gatepost and will be following these all the way round. Keep ahead, ignoring a couple of tracks that come in from the right, and then climb briefly before swinging

> This walk actually follows the **family cycle trail** around the reservoir. Keep your eyes open for the waymark posts that will make navigation easy for you.

round to the left. Continue past a wide turning area and drop down to cross a footbridge that actually spans the infant River Usk **A**.

Climb away from this and continue along what is the most undulating section of the whole walk. You'll soon start to get some views of the water down through the trees to your right and eventually you'll swing round to the right and drop down to the water level, with some fairly bleak looking moorland to your left **B**. There's also a picnic table here, if you fancy stopping a while.

Cross the footbridge and continue uphill until the track turns a sharp right to start heading along the northern shore. This is a lovely section, with the water below you to the right and some rather grand Caledonian pines scattered along the trail. Keep ahead, with great views over the lake, until another waymark finally directs you left, away from the water and uphill slightly **C**.

*Usk Reservoir from the dam*

The **River Usk** rises up from a boggy moorland plateau just a few miles south of the reservoir, in the shadow of the magnificent mountains of the Carmarthen Fan. It drops easily from the bleak moorland to the reservoir forming the boundary between Powys and Carmarthenshire as it goes. From here, the river gains steam again, plummeting over the dam before continuing east past Sennybridge and on to Brecon, where it meanders southwards to divide the Brecon Beacons from the Black Mountains. At Llangynidr it swings east again, running almost parallel with the Monmouthshire and Brecon Canal. This lovely stretch ends at Abergavenny where the Usk is joined by the Gavenny River (see Walk 2). Here, it bears south east and continues over much flatter ground to join the Bristol Channel at Newport.

You'll pass a grassy track coming in from the left but keep on the main cycle trail and you'll shortly reach another junction, where you bear round to the right, to run parallel with the shores once again. Stay with this and you'll cross a small tributary before dropping slowly back to water level close to the ornate building that protrudes into the waters. Keep ahead and go through a barrier to join the tarmac drive and then follow this around to the left and then right, to round the northern tip of the reservoir **D**.

> **?** How many different types of duck can you see on the water?

The drive now cruises along the shore, with a few picnic tables to your right. Pass beneath a large house on your left and continue to the end of

*View from the start looking back over the mountains*

the dam, where you'll see a few small boats moored. Turn right to cross the dam and keep right at the other end to walk through the car park and up the road. This section follows the narrow lane for a few minutes but *while you should obviously take care, it doesn't see much traffic.*

The **Usk Reservoir** lies at just over 1,000ft (305m) above sea level and is the most recent of the Brecon Beacons' reservoirs opening as recently as 1955.

Bear round to the left, ignoring an obvious forest track to your right, and climb slightly to another track on the right, this one marked with the cycle trail signing ⑤. Turn right here and keep ahead at a crossroads of tracks to another, where you should turn left, uphill slightly. Follow this for around 300 yds where it starts to curve round to the right. Stay with it as it drops easily to join another track at the bottom. This is the track that you started on. Turn left onto this and follow it back to the gate and across the road to the car park. ■

# Pen y Fan

- Beacons high point
- memorial
- unbelievable views
- mountain scenery

*walk 20*

*This is the toughest walk in the book, as you'd probably expect from the highest mountain in the National Park. The good news is that it's probably not as tough as you'd expect starting quite high in the first place and following clear paths all the way. The rewards are incredible with views that really do match the satisfaction of the achievement.*

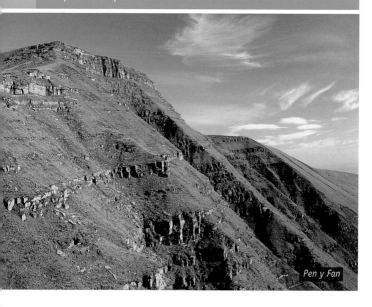

Pen y Fan

**START** Storey Arms

**DISTANCE** 5 miles (8km)

**TIME** 3 hours

**PARKING** At the start.
No charge

**ROUTE FEATURES** Rocky
paths; steep climbs;
mountain summits

**GPS WAYPOINTS**
SN 982 203
Ⓐ SN 992 212
Ⓑ SO 003 214
Ⓒ SO 007 213
Ⓓ SO 012 215
Ⓔ SO 006 209
Ⓕ SN 988 198

**PUBLIC TRANSPORT** Buses
between Brecon and
Merthyr Tydfil, also
summer Beacons Bus
services

**REFRESHMENTS** There's
often a snack van in the
car park

**PUBLIC TOILETS** In the car
park to the south

**PLAY AREA** At the start

**ORDNANCE SURVEY MAPS**
Explorer OL12 (Brecon
Beacons National Park
– Western & Central
areas), Landranger 160
(Brecon Beacons)

Cross the road and go through the gate, next to the telephone box, outside the Storey Arms Outdoor Adventure Centre.

Now follow a clear path up the hillside, leaving the plantation behind and crossing the open moorland that makes up the southern

> ✳ Pen y Fan is usually climbed in a linear, out and back fashion, using the main track used here in descent. The **circular route** described here is a lot more interesting yet not much more difficult.

flanks of Y Gyrn – the bare rounded summit over to your left. You'll soon gain a broad ridge, where you need to cross a stile and drop down to the very infant Taf Fawr River Ⓐ. The way ahead is obvious now, with a clear, rocky, man-made track heading directly up the hillside on the other side of the valley. Follow it until it reaches the steep escarpment edge high above the deeply gouged valley of Cwm Llwch Ⓑ. Far below you'll see the small lake of Llyn y Cwm Llwch and towering above this, you'll see the steep crags of Corn Du.

If you've got the energy, bear left here and drop down the obvious path for about 300 yds, where you'll find the Tommy Jones memorial. Remember that you have to climb back up to this spot afterwards. If you'd rather save your energy, bear right and climb

**Tommy Jones** was a five-year-old miner's son. In August 1900, he visited the area with his father to see his grandfather, who lived on a farm below the peaks. They walked from the old railway station in Brecon and stopped for a rest at a local army camp, where they were met by his grandfather and also his 13-year-old cousin, Willie. The two older men were enjoying the company of the soldiers so decided to stay at the camp for a while. They sent the two boys on ahead to tell Tommy's grandmother of their impending arrival. It was getting quite late and, as it started to get dark, Tommy was scared and decided to return to his father. Willie continued to the farm to tell his grandmother as arranged. Tragically however, Tommy never made it back to the camp.

A huge search ensued. The army became involved and so did the daily newspapers – one actually offering a reward for information. Sadly, weeks went by without any sight of him and then, a local woman dreamed of the boy and led her husband straight up onto a ridge, where she'd never been before, and where they discovered the small boy's body. He had died of exhaustion and exposure. An obelisk now stands close to the spot where his body was found. It was moved a few years ago to reduce erosion.

**? What date did they finally find Tommy Jones?**

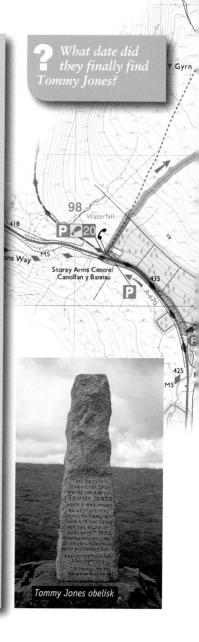

*Tommy Jones obelisk*

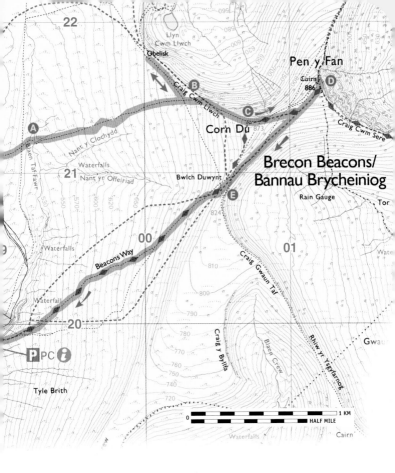

the obvious path steeply up to the rocky ramparts that guard the summit of Corn Du. The table-topped summit is crowned with a sprawling cairn **C**.

The way to Pen y Fan is straightforward now. Drop easily into the shallow notch that separates the two peaks and then climb up onto the highest point in southern Britain. While the summit is flat and, at first glance, not all that exciting, walk over to the precipitous north east face and you'll start to get an idea of the scale and grandeur of this beautiful mountain **D**.

*On the summit of Pen y Fan, Cribyn behind*

To descend, walk back across towards Corn Du and then bear left to follow the obvious track that contours around the summit into the pass on the other side, which is known as Bwlch Duwynt **E**. This is a major junction of paths and you need to take the obvious right-hand one that descends steeply down the hillside towards the A470. Some sections of this have been man-made out of local sandstone to reduce erosion, which is a big problem in these hills.

Follow the track easily down for just over a mile and you'll see the Taf Fawr River down to your right. Continue to a wooden bridge **F** and cross this to go through a kissing-gate and into the main car park. Turn right into the car park and follow the pavement along to the very end, where a broad track takes over and leads through the wood to the A470. Bear right to follow the clear path along the side of the road and then cross by the telephone box to return to the start.

# Further Information

## Safety on the Hills

The hills, mountains and moorlands of Britain, though of modest height compared with those in many other countries, need to be treated with respect. Friendly and inviting in good weather, they can quickly be transformed into wet, misty, windswept and potentially dangerous areas of wilderness in bad weather. Even on an outwardly fine and settled summer day, conditions can rapidly deteriorate. In winter, of course, the weather can be even more erratic and the hours of daylight are much shorter.

Pen y Fan in winter

Therefore it is advisable to always take both warm and waterproof clothing, sufficient nourishing food, a hot drink, first-aid kit, torch and whistle. Wear suitable footwear, such as strong walking boots or shoes that give a good grip over rocky terrain and on slippery slopes. Try to obtain a local weather forecast and bear it in mind before you start. Do not be afraid to abandon your proposed route and return to your starting point in the event of a sudden and unexpected deterioration in the weather. Do not go alone. Allow enough time to finish the walk well before nightfall.

Most of the walks described in this book do not venture into remote wilderness areas and will be safe to do, given due care and respect, at any time of year in all but the most unreasonable weather. Indeed, a crisp, fine winter day often provides perfect walking conditions, with firm ground underfoot and a clarity that is not possible to achieve in the other seasons of the year. A few walks, however, are suitable only for reasonably fit and

*Forest track and trees, Coed Taf Fawr, Garwnant*

Craig Cerrig-Gleisiad

experienced hill walkers able to use a compass and should definitely not
be tackled by anyone else during the winter months or in bad weather,
especially high winds and mist. These are indicated in the general
description that precedes each of the walks.

## Global Positioning System (GPS)
### What is GPS?

Global Positioning System, or GPS for short, is a fully-functional
navigation system that uses a network of satellites to calculate positions,
which are then transmitted to hand-held receivers. By measuring the
time it takes a signal to reach the receiver, the distance from the satellite
can be estimated. Repeat this with several satellites and the receiver can
then triangulate its position, in effect telling the receiver exactly where
you are, in any weather, day or night, anywhere on Earth.

GPS information, in the form of grid reference data, is increasingly being
used in *Pathfinder*® guidebooks, and many readers find the positional

*Rainbow over Glyntawe*

accuracy GPS affords a reassurance, although its greatest benefit comes when you are walking in remote, open countryside or through forests.

GPS has become a vital global utility, indispensable for modern navigation on land, sea and air around the world, as well as an important tool for map-making and land surveying.

**Follow the Country Code**

- Be safe – plan ahead and follow any signs
- Leave gates and property as you find them
- Protect plants and animals, and take your litter home
- Keep dogs under close control
- Consider other people

(Natural England)

## Useful Organisations

**Brecon Beacons National Park Authority**
Plas y Ffynnon, Cambrian Way,
Brecon, Powys
LD3 7HP
Tel. 01874 624437
www.beacons-npa.gov.uk

**CADW Welsh Historic Monuments**
CADW Welsh Assembly
Government, Plas Carew,
Unit 5/7 Cefn Coed,
Parc Nantgarw,
Cardiff CF15 7QQ
Tel. 01443 33 6000
www.cadw.wales.gov.uk

**Campaign for the Protection of Rural Wales**
Tŷ Gwyn, 31 High Street,
Welshpool, Powys
SY21 7YD
Tel. 01938 552525
www.cprw.org.uk

**Coed Cymru**
The Old Sawmill, Tregynon,
Newtown, Powys SY16 3PL
Tel. 01686 650777
www.coedcymru.org.uk

**Countryside Council for Wales**
Maes-y-Ffynnon, Penrhosgarnedd,
Bangor, Gwynedd
LL57 2DW
Tel. 08451 306229
www.ccw.gov.uk

**National Trust office – South Wales**
Gardener's Cottage,
Tredegar House, Newport,
NP10 8YW
Tel. 01633 811659
www.nationaltrust.org.uk

**Ordnance Survey**
Tel. 03456 05 05 05 (Lo-call)
www.ordnancesurvey.co.uk

**Ramblers**
2nd Floor, Camelford House,
87-90 Albert Embankment,
London SE1 7TW
Tel. 020 7339 8500
www.ramblers.org.uk

**Ramblers Wales**
3 Coopers Yard, Curran Road,
Cardiff CF10 5NB
Tel. 029 2064 4308
www.ramblers.org.uk/wales

**Youth Hostel Association (England and Wales) Ltd.**
Trevelyan House, Dimple Road,
Matlock, Derbyshire
DE4 3YH
Tel. 01629 592600
www.yha.org.uk

*Wildlife Trusts in and around the Brecon Beacons:*

**Brecknock Wildlife Trust**
Lion House,
Bethel Square,
Brecon, Powys
LD3 7AY
Tel. 01874 625708
www.brecknockwildlifetrust.org.uk

**Gwent Wildlife Trust**
Seddon House,
Dingestow,
Monmouth
NP25 4DY
Tel. 01600 740600
www.gwentwildlife.org.

**The Wildlife Trust of South and West Wales**
The Nature Centre,
Fountain Road,
Tondu, Bridgend
CF32 0EH
Tel. 01656 724100
www.welshwildlife.org

*Tourist Information Centres:*
**Brecon Tourist Information Office**
Cattle Market Car Park
Brecon
LD3 9DA
Tel. 01874 622485
www.breconbeacons.org/brecon-tourist-information

*Other tourist information centres:*
**Abergavenny**
Tel. 01873 853254

**Crickhowell**
Tel. 01873 811970

**Hay-on-Wye**
Tel. 01497 820144

**Llandovery**
Tel. 01550 720693

**Merthyr Tydfil**
Tel. 01685 727474

**Pont Nedd Fechan**
Tel. 01639 721795

*National Park Visitor Centre:*
**The National Park Visitor Centre**
Brecon, Powys LD3 8ER
Tel. 01874 623366

*Public Transport*
For all public transport enquiries:
**Traveline Cymru**
Tel. 0871 2002233
www.traveline-cymru.info

**National Rail Enquiries**
Tel. 08457 484950

*Ordnance Survey maps of the Brecon Beacons*

**Explorer maps:**  OL12 (Brecon Beacons National Park –
Western & Central areas)
OL13 (Brecon Beacons National Park –
Eastern area)

**Landranger maps:**  160 (Brecon Beacons)
161 (The Black Mountains)

Monmouthshire and Brecon Canal, Gilwern

*Answers to Questions:*

Walk 1:   Three.
Walk 2:   Y Fenni.
Walk 3:   Y Deri Fach.
Walk 4:   They do not lose their leaves in the winter.
Walk 5:   A reservoir is man-made.
Walk 6:   Shire horses.
Walk 7:   Because they are easier to defend.
Walk 8:   An aqueduct.
Walk 9:   ——
Walk 10:  It's called Whitewalls but is actually made of stone and red in colour.
Walk 11:  Nineteen.
Walk 12:  ——
Walk 13:  Six metres.
Walk 14:  Oak trees.
Walk 15:  The middle one, Pen y Fan.
Walk 16:  ——
Walk 17:  Look at the plinth in the car park if you need help.
Walk 18:  England.
Walk 19:  ——
Walk 20:  2 September.

# Crimson Walking Guides

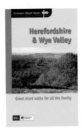

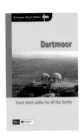
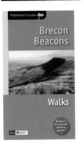
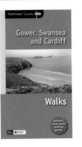

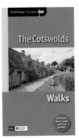
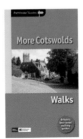
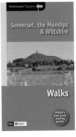

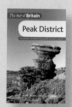